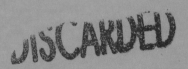

THE
MEATLOAF
BAKERY
COOKBOOK

THE MEATLOAF BAKERY

COOKBOOK

Comfort food with a twist

Cynthia Kallile

Published by
Adams Media, a division of F+W Media, Inc.
57 Littlefield Street, Avon, MA 02322. U.S.A.
www.adamsmedia.com

ISBN-10: 1-4405-4454-9
ISBN-13: 978-1-4405-4454-5
eISBN-10: 1-4405-4455-7
eISBN-13: 978-1-4405-4455-2

Printed in China

Color origination by Ivy Press Reprographics

10 9 8 7 6 5 4 3 2 1

Library of Congress Cataloging-in-Publication Data
is available from the publisher.

This book was conceived, designed, and produced by
Ivy Press
Creative Director Peter Bridgewater
Publisher Susan Kelly
Commissioning Editor Sophie Collins
Editorial Director Tom Kitch
Art Director James Lawrence
Designer Karen Wilks
Editor Jo Richardson
Food Photographer Clive Streeter
Home Economist Teresa Goldfinch
Location Photographer Rob Streeter

This book uses imperial, metric, and US cup measurements. Follow the same units
of measurement throughout; do not mix imperial and metric. All spoon and cup
measurements are level: 1 teaspoon is assumed to be 5 ml, 1 tablespoon is assumed
to be 15 ml, and 1 cup is assumed to be 250 ml.

Always follow safety and commonsense cooking protocol while using kitchen utensils,
operating ovens and stoves, and handling uncooked food. If children are assisting in the
preparation of any recipe, they should always be supervised by an adult.

*This book is available at quantity discounts for bulk purchases. For information,
please call 1-800-289-0963.*

Contents

THE MEATLOAF BAKERY STORY

I love it when people ask me if I always dreamed of having a meatloaf business. "Of course," I answer. Who wouldn't? After all, isn't meatloaf one of the classic All-American dishes? It's the perfect comfort food and often brings back memories of Mom's cooking.

For me, those memories are very special. As a child helping my mother in the kitchen, I had no idea that one day I'd be showcasing her absolutely delicious meatloaf in my very own store. Yet somewhere deep inside I must have known I'd be celebrating her lovely relationship with cooking and delighting others through food in my own way.

Although I worked in corporate public relations for 25 years, food was never far from my mind. Taking whatever I had on hand either from the farmer's market or the grocery store, I would prepare something in the evening while watching TV or listening to Barbra Streisand. I loved coming up with new recipes, feverishly scribbling them into my journal if they were good.

But changing careers in midlife—what was I thinking? Why meatloaf? For me, preparing meatloaf was a way to be creative and take risks in the kitchen—to test my ability to put ingredients together in an irresistible way, and to create something that would not only bring back memories of home, but also create new memories for everyone who tasted it.

For three years, I planned, cooked, and experimented with the help of many dear friends, relatives, and meatloaf fans. From endless varieties of meats, vegetables, sauces, condiments, and grains, new twists on classic recipes were born. But the recipes weren't quite perfect; something was still missing. Why can't meatloaf be pretty? It can, and the icing on the cake turned out to be meatloaf's favorite sidekick, mashed potatoes. Now meatloaf would not only be delicious, but beautiful, too. I set out to create works of art in many appetizing pastry shapes and forms, such as cupcakes, cakes, pies, and even bite-size appetizers, each topped with a special blend of potatoes, pasta, or veggies.

The Mother Loaf, in honor of my mom, was the heart of all good things to come. The Meatloaf Bakery opened in December 2008, and since then it has grown to be a Chicago favorite for natives and tourists alike. As home of the original meatloaf cupcake, we continue to delight customers in our store and from our food truck, Meatloaf-A-Go-Go.

Now, with this book, we bring the best of what we do to you—recipes for memorable meals, reminders of good food we grew up with, and inspiration to be creative in your own kitchen.

INGREDIENTS MAKE THE LOAF

You can't create a meatloaf, or a meatless loaf for that matter, without key ingredients, namely meats, poultry, fish, eggs, dairy, veggies, herbs, and spices—plus, of course, those always-important bread or cracker crumbs.

MEATS

Whether you buy them ground or choose to grind them yourself, fresh quality meats are essential when creating any one of my meatloaf recipes. Although I recommend the traditional combination of beef, pork, and veal for a classic-style meatloaf, you may select any blend of these three primary meats.

Ground chuck is my meat of choice in the beef category. It is 80 to 85% lean, so it's ideal for the perfect meatloaf, with just enough fat to enhance the flavor and prevent dryness. Ground veal is helpful for adding smoothness to the mix.

Ground pork is simply that—all pork and nothing else. Typically, Italian sausage or chorizo is made from pork with extra seasonings, however turkey and chicken varieties are available, too, and you can find these in specialty markets.

Lamb, also ground, is a delicious addition to the world of meatloaf recipes, but it needs to be tender and fresh, so check with your butcher if you're uncertain about making the right choice.

POULTRY AND SEAFOOD

Ground turkey and chicken are readily available in most grocery stores. I prefer a combination of both light and dark meat for enhanced flavor and moisture. If you'd like to reduce your calories and fat a bit, you may choose all white meat, although dark meat is claimed to contain more nutrients and vitamins—so why not go for a blend?

Salmon is best fresh, but frozen can be used—just be sure to thaw it out in the refrigerator before preparing. I opt for wild-caught Alaskan, but any variety will work, depending upon your preference and budget. You may also choose canned white or light tuna packed in water.

THE FILLER

I generally use bread crumbs, crushed butter crackers, or the occasional oyster cracker for this purpose. The bread crumbs are mostly the dry, unseasoned white variety, unless otherwise specified in the recipe ingredients list. Store-bought work just fine, but if you prefer to make your own it's simple: just crumble dry (not stale) bread into fine crumbs, either by hand or using a food processor. If you have only fresh bread, you can easily dry it by placing crust-free slices on an ungreased cookie sheet and baking at 300°F/150°C, turning once, for approximately 10 to 15 minutes until they are dry. Panko bread crumbs (found in most specialty or Asian markets) also add texture and a lighter touch to many recipes. Last, but certainly not least, are the tried and true rolled oats— I choose 100% whole grain, but in any event make sure you avoid the instant variety.

EGGS AND DAIRY

Eggs hold ingredients together, and dairy products create moisture to make delicious juicy meatloaf. Use large eggs, not medium or jumbo. All my recipes recommend 2% milk, but if you prefer you may use whole milk for a richer outcome or nonfat milk for an even healthier alternative. Some recipes include sour cream, plain yogurt, whipping cream, or buttermilk, but there's no need to skimp on these unless you must for dietary or health purposes. When a recipe calls for butter, use unsalted unless otherwise specified. If you do use salted butter, slightly reduce the salt amounts in the recipe.

FRESH VEGETABLES, FRUITS, AND HERBS

Just about every recipe in this book calls for some type of fresh vegetable, herb, or fruit juice. All are easily found at a grocery store, specialty market, or perhaps in your garden. Whether it's red bell peppers, lemons, celery, carrots, or onions, be sure to wash or peel them well (as appropriate) before slicing, dicing, or juicing. Most of these ingredients can be prepared ahead of time, covered with plastic wrap, and refrigerated.

Fresh herbs are my preference, but several of my recipes call for dried herbs; I believe there's a place for both in every kitchen. If you love the smell of fresh basil, rosemary, thyme, or mint, pick up small herb plants and enjoy them year-round, either in flowerpots placed on a sunny kitchen windowsill or outdoors, depending on season or climate.

To Be or Not to Be a Cupcake

Each of the meatloaf recipes in this cookbook has been created in a unique bakery-inspired form. From cupcakes, loaves, and cakes to pies and even logs, most are interchangeable, so feel free to experiment with the various shapes and recipes. When it's time to choose a garnish, topping, or accompaniment for the final dish, that, too, can be up to you, but ideal combinations are suggested.

TOOLS AND TECHNIQUES MAKE THE LOAF

To me, the beauty of meatloaf and all its variations is that, generally speaking, it's very forgiving. If you don't have time to lightly beat the eggs, don't worry. If you add a little too much ketchup, no one will notice because, after all, just about everyone loves ketchup. Yet there are a few handy tools, steps, and tips that will make your kitchen experience even more fulfilling.

READY, PREP, GO!

Hand chopping can be oh-so therapeutic, so give it a whirl if time permits. Just be sure to use a sharp knife with a wide blade, such as a chef's knife. Alternatively, try a mezzaluna—this amazing single- or double-blade knife is curved like a halfmoon and perfect for hand chopping.

Useful Equipment
The following items aren't essential, but you may find them helpful in preparing some of the recipes:

- food processor
- immersion blender
- ice-cream scoop
- lemon juicer
- mortar and pestle
- salad spinner
- wire whisk
- instant-read thermometer

Pots and Pans for Baking

The specific baking pans you need will, of course, depend on which recipes you choose to make. The following list covers every form of meatloaf the recipes take: loaf, cupcake, pie, layer cake, sheet cake, and potpie:

- two nonstick 10-inch x 5-inch/ 25-cm x 13-cm loaf pans
- large (not jumbo) and regular nonstick 6-cup cupcake/muffin pan
- nonstick 9-inch/23-cm or 10-inch/25-cm pie pan
- two nonstick 8-inch/20-cm round cake pans
- eight large (9–10-oz./250–280-g) ramekins
- 13-inch x 9-inch x 2-inch/ 5-cm x 23-cm x 5-cm baking pan
- 12-inch x 9-inch/30-cm x 23-cm baking dish
- 9-inch x 7-inch/23-cm x 18-cm baking dish
- 8-inch x 8-inch/20-cm x 20-cm baking pan
- nonstick cookie sheet or sheet pan
- assorted sauté pans, saucepans, and stock pots

Parsley

Do take care with curly parsley, because it can be rather dirty. I recommend, and my mother insists, that it be picked from the stems first so you have only the curly flowerlike ends. Place the parsley in a salad spinner filled with cold water. Soak and rinse it two or three times to be sure the water is clean—sometimes adding a shake of salt to the water can help separate the dirt from the parsley. Use the salad spinner to spin out the water. Lay the fresh-picked parsley on paper towels and pat lightly with paper towels to dry thoroughly—the drier the better. If you're up for chopping, grab your favorite chef's knife and a cutting board and chop away. If you're not up for it, then use a food processor.

Thyme

Fresh thyme is a delightful herb and I use it often in my recipes. I know it takes "thyme," but be sure to remove the tiny green leaves from the woody stems. Then you'll just need to chop it quickly and add to the mixture.

Basil

Fresh basil is one of the easier herbs to prepare. Give it a quick rinse if need be and pat it dry with paper towels. Pick the leaves from the stems and briskly chop by hand. For recipes requiring a lot of chopped basil, you can use a food processor.

Garlic

Fresh garlic is a staple in my kitchen. Easily purchased as bulbs or in containers of individual peeled cloves, garlic adds so much to so many recipes. Remove the ends from each clove before chopping. Now here's a tip for smashing garlic learned in one Toledo, Ohio, kitchen circa 1964. Grab a small bowl and place a little salt in the bottom of it (salt acts as an abrasive and helps draw out the juices). Add the garlic clove(s) and, using the end of a wooden knife handle or pestle, smash the garlic to a fine paste.

Lemons

For a fast spritz of lemon juice, holding half a lemon in one hand, use your other hand to insert a table fork into the lemon's flesh and squeeze the lemon around it to release the juice. It's as good as a stress ball, and much tastier. Remember to remove the seeds with a mesh strainer.

MASTERING THE MIX

My favorite part in preparing meatloaf is mixing. It's the culmination of prepping all those ingredients, bringing everything together—the colors, aromas, and flavors. I recommend mixing everything by hand, although you may use a mixer or food processor, but be careful to avoid overmixing—you need to only thoroughly blend the ingredients, and too much mixing can make your meatloaf tough or possibly dry.

After blending your meatloaf mixture, place it in the prepared loaf, cupcake, pie, or cake pan. Shape the mixture as directed in the recipe and smooth the top with your hands or a cake spatula. Be sure to distribute the mixture evenly and give the pan a gentle tap or two on the counter to settle it.

If you've made more than one batch of the recipe and would like to bake it at a later time, wrap the raw mixture in foil or plastic wrap and store in the refrigerator, or freeze it if you plan to keep it longer than a day. When you're ready to bake it, simply follow the recipe baking instructions. If your raw meatloaf mixture has been in the freezer, either first thaw it in the refrigerator and then bake it once it's thoroughly thawed, or place it directly in the oven without thawing and add 20 to 30 extra minutes of baking time.

Meatloaf Memos
- Read the recipe thoroughly.
- Preheat the oven to 375°F/190°C.
- Prepare all your ingredients and set them up for easy access.
- Prepare your pans by greasing them with canola or vegetable oil spray.
- Make sure your instant-read thermometer is calibrated correctly.
- Be sure to wash your cutting boards after each use to avoid cross-contamination.
- Turn on your favorite music and enjoy the process!

FROM OVEN TO TABLE

This phase of the meatloaf journey is easy, especially if you follow a few simple guidelines.

Be sure your oven reaches the desired temperature before you use it. While the cooking times in each recipe are good estimates, I recommend using an instant-read thermometer to ensure the item is cooked properly but not overcooked—160°F/71°C for meat, seafood, and vegetarian mixtures, or 165°F/74°C for poultry. About halfway through the cooking time, turn the pan around.

After removing the meatloaf from the oven, carefully drain off any liquid that may have accumulated in the pan. Once cool enough to handle (about 7 to 10 minutes), run a knife or cake spatula around the edge of the pan to release the meatloaf. An unmolding technique that works well for me is to lay a small cutting board over the meatloaf pan and, while holding the board and pan together, flip the board and pan over so the meatloaf comes out onto the cutting board. From here you can garnish or top the meatloaf with potatoes, vegetables, or whatever the recipe calls for.

Just about all my recipes can be made ahead of time, refrigerated, and reheated. In fact, I recommend this method in particular if assembling a two-layer meatloaf cake, as follows:

1. Bake the two single meatloaf layers.

2. Unmold and refrigerate.

3. Follow the directions for the "cake filling and frosting."

4. Assemble and refrigerate until ready to heat and serve.

5. Place in the oven for approximately 45 minutes, or until the internal temperature reaches 165°F/74°C. Cover with aluminum foil, if necessary, to prevent overbrowning.

FROM FREEZER TO OVEN

Completely cooked meatloaf also freezes very well. After your meatloaf is thoroughly cooled, wrap and label it clearly, and then place in the freezer—it will be ready when you are. There's no need to first thaw it, but if you prefer, do so in the refrigerator. Otherwise simply slip it into an oven preheated to 375°F/190°C, cover with aluminum foil, and bake for 20 to 30 minutes, then remove the foil and cook for another 20 to 30 minutes, or until the internal temperature reaches 165°F/74°C.

THE POTATO DE RESISTANCE

So why can't meatloaf be pretty? I think it can, and that's the magic of these recipes. By pairing scrumptious meatloaf with creative toppings and garnishes, such as potatoes, cheesy crumbles, pasta, or colorful bell peppers, tasty yet otherwise unexciting meatloaf is transformed into a work of art. So have fun and be creative with your finishing touches.

Piping potatoes can be somewhat challenging, but if you carefully follow these few steps, it should turn out picture perfect. Star pastry tips are easy to use, and you can also view videos demonstrating piping techniques online.

1. Insert your chosen pastry tip into the pastry bag.

2. Fill the bag halfway with the prepared potatoes.

3. Hold the bag upright and squeeze gently but firmly to release the potatoes. Use caution, because the bag may be hot to the touch; if too hot to handle, hold with a pot holder or a towel.

Scooping potatoes (or prepared rice) is a simple and fun alternative. Any ice-cream scoop will work. And when you're in a hurry, just place the potatoes or any topping on your meatloaf with a cake spatula or your hands. Only watch out for those hot potatoes!

Potato "Frosting" Supplies
- 12–14-inch/30–35-cm pastry bags (disposable, reusable, or silicone)
- stainless-steel star pastry tips or any tip wide enough for prepared mashed potatoes to pass through (you can purchase cake-decorating kits that include an assortment of bags and tips)
- pot holder/towel in case the potatoes are too hot to handle in the pastry bag
- ice-cream scoop for scooping
- cake spatula for spreading

A DAY IN
THE LIFE
OF THE
MEATLOAF
BAKERY

The Meatloaf
Bakery

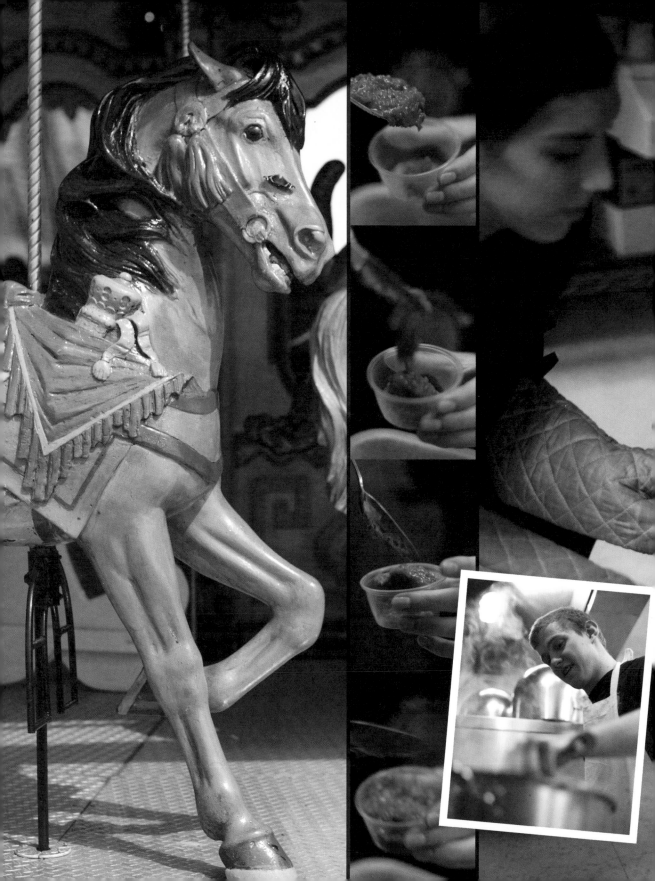

Living The Meatloaf Bakery life starts each day with the preparation. Whether it's gearing up for a luncheon, stocking our food truck, Meatloaf-A-Go-Go, or just planning for the day, there are cheeses to shred, sauces to portion, vegetables to roast, and potatoes to mash. And of course, meatloaf to make!

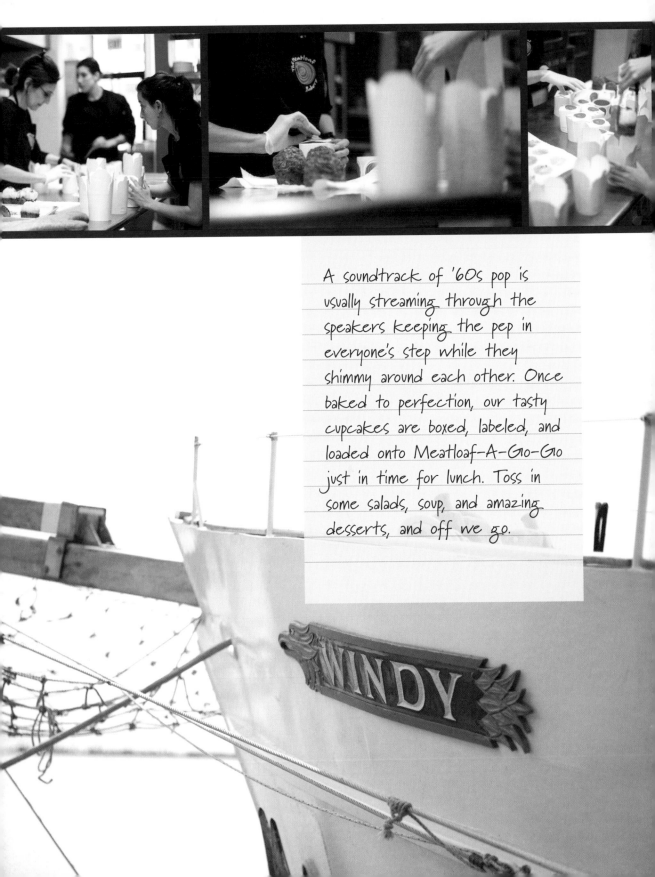

A soundtrack of '60s pop is usually streaming through the speakers keeping the pep in everyone's step while they shimmy around each other. Once baked to perfection, our tasty cupcakes are boxed, labeled, and loaded onto Meatloaf-A-Go-Go just in time for lunch. Toss in some salads, soup, and amazing desserts, and off we go.

A standout among food trucks, Meatloaf-A-Go-Go hits the streets carrying our signature meatloaf cupcakes. Each day we pick a new destination and tweet our whereabouts to our fans. And what do we love? Sold out! See you all tomorrow! Meanwhile, back in the store, the day's prep is now in high gear as we prepare to open.

Quite often, as soon as we lock the door behind our departing Meatloaf-A-Go-Go driver and turn back to our cooking, there's a knock on the door. An early bird gazes hungrily into our storefront at our beautiful display of savory cupcakes, Loafies, and sides. No turning away this hungry customer.

Most days, we are a well-oiled, meatloaf-making machine. But all it takes is one last-minute catering order or request for a special meatloaf birthday cake to make things crazy in the kitchen. We live for days like these though, as there's nothing more exhilarating than customers clamoring for our beautiful and delicious meatloaf.

Making and decorating meatloaf our way every day is unbelievably fun and rewarding. But it's serious business—we take care and pride in every detail, from choosing just the right combination of ingredients to putting on that finishing touch of dill. We love it, and we work hard to share our enthusiasm with our customers.

MEATLOAF CLASSICS

From The Mother Loaf and Herby Turkey Loaf to A Loaf in Every Pot (Pie) and No Buns About It Burger Loaf, one of a kind variations on comfort food favorites. All with sauces and sides to match.

THE MOTHER LOAF

Servings: 6

This is where it all started—my mom's "recipe," although she claims she never had a formal recipe. And I believe it because that's how she cooked. I recalled how delicious her meatloaf was, so I created this version from memory. I've included a little green pepper, but that's optional. Top it with Yukon Smashers and enjoy it with Demiglace. You'll definitely please everyone with The Mother Loaf, including your mother.

TO MAKE

- Preheat the oven to 375°F/190°C.

- In a bowl, combine the onion, celery, bell peppers, condiments, herbs, paprika, and seasonings. In a separate bowl, combine the oats, butter cracker crumbs, milk, and eggs with the ground meats. Add the vegetable mixture and mix well with your hands.

- Place the meatloaf mixture in a greased nonstick 10-inch x 5-inch/25-cm x 13-cm loaf pan and smooth the top with your hands or a cake spatula. Bake in the oven for about 45 to 50 minutes, or until the internal temperature reaches 160°F/71°C and the top is browned. Remove from the oven and let cool for a few minutes.

- While the meatloaf is baking and cooling slightly, prepare the Yukon Smashers, following the recipe on page 124.

- When cool enough to handle, unmold the meatloaf carefully and set aside as you prepare for the crowning touch. Insert any pastry tip into a 12 to 14-inch/30 to 35-cm pastry bag and fill with the hot Yukon Smashers (use caution, because the bag can be hot to the touch). Be creative and make any design you'd like on top of the loaf. If you're going for a more traditional look, just spread your potatoes on top of the loaf and sprinkle with fresh parsley. Serve with Demiglace (see page 152).

For the Meatloaf

- 1 cup finely diced yellow onion
- ½ cup finely diced celery
- ¼ cup finely diced red bell pepper
- ¼ cup finely diced green bell pepper (optional)
- ¼ cup plus 2 tbsp. ketchup
- 2 tbsp. Worcestershire sauce
- 2 tsp. prepared yellow mustard
- ⅔ cup chopped fresh curly or Italian parsley, plus extra for topping (optional)
- 1 tsp. finely chopped fresh thyme leaves
- ½ tsp. dried marjoram
- 1 tsp. paprika
- ½ tsp. seasoned salt
- ½ tsp. coarse sea salt
- 1 tsp. black pepper
- 1 cup 100% whole grain rolled oats
- 1 cup butter cracker crumbs
- ⅔ cup 2% milk
- 2 large eggs, lightly beaten
- ⅓ lb./300 g ground chuck beef
- ⅓ lb./300 g ground pork
- ⅓ lb./300 g ground veal
- canola or vegetable oil spray, for greasing
- 1 batch Yukon Smashers (see page 124), for topping
- Demiglace (see page 152), for serving

THE FATHER LOAF

Servings: 6 to 8

If you're going to have The Mother Loaf, you've got to have The Father Loaf. So what makes this meatloaf different from its better half? You'll see. We've added some barbecue sauce, a different herb blend, and topped it with Cheesy Taters. Here's to dads everywhere!

For the Meatloaf
1 cup dry white bread crumbs
1 cup 100% whole grain rolled oats
⅔ cup 2% milk
⅓ cup ketchup
1 tbsp. plus 2 tsp. Worcestershire sauce
2 tsp. traditional barbecue sauce
2 tsp. minced garlic
2 tsp. minced fresh chives
1 tsp. dried Herbes de Provence
1 tsp. paprika
1 tsp. fine sea salt
1 tsp. black pepper
1 lb./450 g ground chuck beef
1 lb./450 g ground pork
½ cup finely chopped yellow onion
⅓ cup finely diced celery
¼ cup finely diced red bell pepper
⅔ cup finely chopped curly parsley
2 large eggs, lightly beaten
canola or vegetable oil spray, for greasing
1 batch Cheesy Taters (see page 128), for topping (or Garlic Spuds, see page 126, or Yukon Smashers, see page 124, and ketchup or prepared demiglace, if creating a football-shape meatloaf)

For the Glaze and Dipping Sauce
½ cup ketchup
⅓ cup traditional barbecue sauce
granulated sugar, to taste

TO MAKE

• Preheat the oven to 375°F/190°C.

• Combine the bread crumbs, oats, and milk in a bowl and let soften.

• In a separate bowl, combine the ketchup, Worcestershire and barbecue sauces, garlic, chives, Herbes de Provence, paprika, salt, and pepper. In a large bowl, combine the ground meats, onion, celery, bell pepper, and parsley. Add the eggs, the ketchup mixture, and the softened bread crumb/oats mixture, and then mix well with your hands.

• Cover a sheet pan or cookie sheet with parchment paper and lightly spray with canola or vegetable oil. Using your hands, form the meatloaf mixture into a generous log on the prepared pan and smooth the surface, or create your own shape—Dad may even want to fashion it into a football to accompany one of those big games! Bake in the oven for approximately 35 minutes.

• While the meatloaf is baking, begin preparing the Cheesy Taters, following the recipe on page 128. Also, stir together the ingredients for the glaze and dipping sauce.

• Remove the meatloaf from the oven and brush the top with some of the glaze mixture. Return to the oven and bake for an additional 15 minutes, or until the internal temperature reaches 160°F/71°C, but note that the total cooking time may vary depending on the thickness of your particular creation.

• Top with the hot Cheesy Taters and enjoy with the remaining glaze mixture as a dipping sauce. If you've created a football-shape meatloaf, "frost" it with Garlic Spuds (see page 126 or Yukon Smashers (see page 124), and create football laces with ketchup or prepared demiglace powder (available from some culinary specialty stores and online; follow the package instructions).

MEATLOAF #641

Servings: 6

Sometimes the best recipes come from "oops, we forgot something." That's the case with this special I affectionately call Meatloaf #641. Combining fresh beef, plenty of cheese and onions, and topped with a Tabasco-ketchup glaze and a scoop of Garlic Spuds, it's a great summer meatloaf. Try reheating it on a gas or charcoal grill for an extra dose of summer flavor.

TO MAKE

- First roast the garlic for the Garlic Spuds, following the recipe on page 126. Reduce the oven to 375°F/190°C.

- Heat the canola oil in a small frying pan and cook the onion until softened. Drain on paper towels and cool. In a large bowl, combine all the remaining meatloaf ingredients, add the cooled onions, and mix well with your hands.

- Divide the meatloaf mixture into 6 portions and place in a lightly greased nonstick 6-cup cupcake/muffin pan. Round the top of each meatloaf cupcake with your hands to form a dome. Bake in the oven for approximately 15 minutes. Remove from the oven, mix together the ketchup and Tabasco for the glaze, and brush some of the mixture over the tops of the cupcakes; reserve the remainder for serving. Return to the oven and bake for an additional 15 minutes, or until the internal temperature reaches 160°F/71°C. Remove from the oven and let cool for a few minutes.

- While the meatloaf cupcakes are baking, finish preparing the Garlic Spuds following the recipe on page 126—because they will be scooped onto the cupcakes instead of being piped, they don't need to be quite so smooth.

- Unmold the meatloaf cupcakes carefully and place a scoop of Garlic Spuds on top of each. Decorate with your favorite garnish—grape tomatoes, shredded cheese, or bacon bits— and serve with the remaining glaze mixture on the side.

For the Meatloaf
1 batch Garlic Spuds (see page 126), for topping
1 tbsp. canola oil
¾ cup plus 1 tbsp. finely diced yellow onion
1½ lb./680 g ground chuck beef
1 cup fine fresh French bread crumbs (see page 9)
1 cup shredded sharp yellow cheddar cheese
1 cup shredded Monterey Jack cheese
½ cup drained and finely diced dill pickles
1 large egg, lightly beaten
¼ cup 2% milk
¼ cup ketchup
2 tbsp. mayonnaise
1 tsp. prepared yellow mustard
⅛ tsp. Tabasco sauce
¾ tsp. coarse sea salt
½ tsp. black pepper
canola or vegetable oil spray, for greasing
grape tomatoes, shredded cheese, or bacon bits, for garnishing

For the Glaze
2 cups ketchup
1 tsp. Tabasco sauce

NO BUNS ABOUT IT BURGER LOAF

Servings: 6

What's a meatloaf store without a meatloaf that tastes just like an All-American bacon-cheddar cheeseburger? Our frequent "Loafers" simply love this recipe, because it blends the best of a cheeseburger with my favorite condiments—dill pickles and mustard. Top it off with some really cheesy potatoes and you've got a winner that kids and adults will love. Enjoy this crowd-pleaser hot from the oven.

TO MAKE

- Preheat the oven to 375°F/190°C.

- Cook the bacon in a frying pan until crisp. Remove with a spatula and set aside. Pour off most of the bacon grease, leaving just enough to coat the bottom of the pan. (This step ensures the onions will absorb just a little of the flavorful bacon grease.) Add the onion and cook for a few minutes until softened. Set aside and cool.

- In a bowl, combine the cooled bacon and onion with all the remaining meatloaf ingredients. Mix well with your hands—be sure to blend everything together, scraping the side of the bowl with a cake spatula to capture every bit of goodness.

- Divide the meatloaf mixture into 6 portions and place in a lightly greased, large nonstick 6-cup cupcake/muffin pan. Round the top of each meatloaf cupcake with your hands to form a dome. Bake in the oven for approximately 30 to 40 minutes, or until the internal temperature reaches 160°F/71°C and the cupcake tops are browned. Remove from the oven and let cool for a few minutes.

- While the meatloaf cupcakes are baking and cooling slightly, prepare the Cheesy Taters, following the recipe on page 128.

- When cool enough to handle, unmold the meatloaf cupcakes carefully and set on a flat surface in preparation for "frosting." Insert any pastry tip into a 12 to 14-inch/30 to 35-cm pastry bag and fill with the hot Cheesy Taters (use caution, because the bag can be hot to the touch). Be creative and make any design you'd like on the cupcakes. No time for artistry? In that case, just spread the potatoes on the top. Sprinkle with cheddar cheese, pickles, and sesame seeds for the real burger experience, then serve with TMB Special Sauce (see page 150).

For the Meatloaf
8 oz./225 g bacon, cut into
    small pieces
¾ cup finely diced yellow onion
1½ lb./680 g ground chuck beef
1 cup dry white bread crumbs
1 cup shredded yellow cheddar cheese,
    plus extra for topping
1 cup shredded Monterey Jack cheese
¼ cup drained and finely diced dill
    pickles, plus extra for topping
1 large egg, lightly beaten
¼ cup 2% milk
¼ cup ketchup
2 tbsp. mayonnaise
1 tsp. prepared yellow mustard
¾ tsp. coarse sea salt
½ tsp. black pepper
canola or vegetable oil spray,
    for greasing
TMB Special Sauce, for serving
    (see page 150)

For the Topping
1 batch Cheesy Taters (see page 128)
sesame seeds, for sprinkling

DOG GONE IT LOAF

Servings: 10

Chicagoans and visitors love a Chicago-style hot dog—savory, salty, beefy goodness in a steamed poppy seed bun. The Meatloaf Bakery's tribute to the famous Windy City hot dog is so darn close that you'll think you're eating the real thing. Shh . . . don't tell anyone that we added a little ketchup to the recipe—a no-no for native Chicagoans.

For the Meatloaf
¾ lb./340 g ground chuck beef
¾ lb./340 g ground pork
1 cup finely diced yellow onion
½ cup finely diced celery
1 tbsp. plus 2 tsp. minced garlic
½ cup drained and finely diced banana
    peppers (from a jar)
½ cup drained and finely diced dill
    pickles, plus extra for topping
2 tbsp. sweet pickle relish
1½ cups dry white bread crumbs
¾ cup shredded sharp yellow
    cheddar cheese
2 large eggs, lightly beaten
½ cup ketchup
2 tbsp. prepared yellow mustard,
    plus extra for topping
1½ tsp. celery salt
1 tsp. black pepper
canola or vegetable oil spray,
    for greasing
hot dog buns, for serving (optional)

For the Topping
1 batch Yukon Smashers (see
    page 124), plus an extra 1 batch
    for serving (optional)
poppy seeds, for sprinkling

TO MAKE

- Preheat the oven to 375°F/190°C.

- In a large bowl, combine the ground meats and then add all the remaining meatloaf ingredients. Mix well with your hands—be sure to blend everything together, scraping the side of the bowl with a cake spatula.

- Cover a sheet pan or cookie sheet with parchment paper and lightly spray with canola or vegetable oil. Divide the meatloaf mixture into 10 portions, form into individual logs about 6 inches/15 cm long and the approximate diameter of a plump hot dog, and place on the prepared pan. Bake in the oven for approximately 20 to 30 minutes, or until the internal temperature reaches 160°F/71°C and the meatloaf logs are browned.

- While the meatloaf logs are baking, prepare the Yukon Smashers, following the recipe on page 124.

- Remove the cooked "dogs" from the oven. Insert any pastry tip into a 12 to 14-inch/30 to 35-cm pastry bag and fill with the hot Yukon Smashers (use caution, because the bag can be hot to the touch). Pipe the potatoes onto your "dogs," then top with a squiggle of mustard, extra dill pickles, and a sprinkling of poppy seeds. Enjoy immediately with an extra helping of Yukon Smashers, or snuggle them into your favorite hot dog buns.

J. P. REUBEN LOAF

Servings: 6 to 8

Dating back to the early 1900s, the Reuben Sandwich has been a cornerstone of American cuisine and is beloved by power-lunching would-be J. P. Morgans and by my own nephew, John Philip (J. P.). We've taken the much-loved combination of corned beef, sauerkraut, Swiss cheese, Thousand Island dressing, and rye bread and put our own twist on it. Hot with Caraway-Horseradish Smashers or between toasted, marble rye slices, this meatloaf is sure to make you fall in love with the famous Reuben again.

TO MAKE

- First prepare the corned beef. Place it in a large Dutch oven, cover with cold water, and bring to a boil. Reduce the heat and simmer for about 2½ hours. Remove from the water, pat dry, and let cool (enough to handle), then cut into small pieces. Pulse lightly in a food processor until you have "ground" corned beef.

- Preheat the oven to 375°F/190°C.

- For the dressing, mix together all the ingredients in a bowl and taste to make sure it's just right—you can increase or decrease any of the quantities to your liking.

- In a bowl, mix together the ground corned beef and chuck beef thoroughly with your hands. Add all the remaining meatloaf ingredients with ½ cup of the Thousand Island dressing and mix well to be sure everything is well distributed.

- Place the meatloaf mixture in a greased nonstick 10-inch x 5-inch/25-cm x 13-cm loaf pan and smooth the top with your hands or a cake spatula. Bake in the oven for approximately 45 to 50 minutes, or until the internal temperature reaches 160°F/71°C and the top is browned. Remove from the oven and let cool for a few minutes.

- While the meatloaf is baking and cooling slightly, prepare the Caraway-Horseradish Smashers, following the recipe on page 128.

- When cool enough to handle, unmold the meatloaf carefully and set on a flat surface in preparation for "frosting." Insert any pastry tip into a 12 to 14-inch/30 to 35-cm pastry bag and fill with the hot Caraway-Horseradish Smashers (use caution, because the bag can be hot to the touch). Make the design of your choice on the top, or, if you're in a rush, just spread the hot potatoes on top of the loaf. Slice and serve hot. Alternatively, you may want to forgo the potatoes and serve slices of the Reuben Loaf (either hot or cold) on toasted marble rye with more Swiss cheese and sauerkraut and the remaining Thousand Island dressing.

For the Meatloaf

1-lb./450-g piece corned beef
8 oz./225 g ground chuck beef
2 cups fresh deli rye bread crumbs (see page 9)
¾ cup drained and rinsed sauerkraut, plus extra for serving (optional)
¼ cup shredded Swiss cheese, plus extra for serving (optional)
2 large eggs, lightly beaten
½ tsp. ground coriander
½ tsp. caraway seeds
½ tsp. black pepper
canola or vegetable oil, for greasing
1 batch Caraway–Horseradish Smashers (see page 128) or toasted marble rye bread slices, for serving

Thousand Island Dressing

½ cup ketchup
½ cup mayonnaise
2 tbsp. sweet pickle relish

THE SISTER LOAF

Servings: 6 to 8

A special recipe in my family is roasted pork with a currant and dry mustard glaze. This tasty sensation replicates beautifully in a meatloaf. Savory and sweet, The Sister Loaf is a tribute to this outstanding recipe. Enjoy it hot with extra glaze and roasted root vegetables and potatoes, or cold between two slices of sourdough bread.

For the Meatloaf
1 cup currant jelly
1 tsp. dry mustard
1½ lb./680 g ground pork
1 cup 100% whole grain rolled oats
1 cup butter cracker crumbs
½ cup chopped yellow onion
½ cup finely diced celery
¼ cup crushed dried rosemary
3 tbsp. minced garlic
1 tsp. finely grated lemon zest
2 large eggs, lightly beaten
1 tsp. coarse sea salt
½ tsp. black pepper
canola or vegetable oil spray,
    for greasing

For the Currant Jelly Glaze
½ cup currant jelly
1 tsp. crushed dried rosemary
1 tsp. crushed garlic (optional)
½ tsp. dry mustard
fine sea salt and black pepper

TO MAKE

• Preheat the oven to 375°F/190°C.

• Mix together the currant jelly and dry mustard and set aside. In a large bowl, combine the pork with all the remaining meatloaf ingredients and the currant jelly and mustard mixture. Mix well with your hands.

• Shape the meatloaf mixture into a freeform loaf shape (like a mound) with your hands in a greased 12-inch x 9-inch/30-cm x 23-cm baking dish and smooth the surface. Bake in the oven for approximately 35 minutes.

• While the meatloaf is baking, prepare the currant jelly glaze. Mix together the currant jelly and dry mustard in a bowl, then add the rosemary and season with salt and pepper. If you want to serve extra glaze on the side, make a double batch.

• Remove the meatloaf from the oven and brush the top with the glaze mixture. Return the loaf to the oven and bake for an additional 15 minutes, or until the internal temperature reaches 160°/71°CF. Slice and serve with the extra currant jelly glaze, if you've made some.

Currant jelly is a classic with pork, and is one of those sweet/savory combinations that works across the board. Early jelly preserves were made exclusively to be eaten with meat (and were often made with boiled-down meat juices), so perhaps it's not surprising that the link has lived on through the years.

HERBY TURKEY LOAF

Servings: 6 to 8

Turkey loaf is popular because it represents an alternative to the more traditional red meat options. However, it can be somewhat bland, so I set out to create a recipe that would be loaded with flavor, texture, and nutrition. And nothing goes better with turkey than dressing (or stuffing as many refer to it) and a side of fresh cranberry sauce. This favorite from The Meatloaf Bakery will soon become a staple on your plate.

TO MAKE

- Preheat the oven to 375°F/190°C.

- Mix together the dried herbs and seasonings in a bowl and set aside. In a separate bowl, combine all the remaining meatloaf ingredients—be sure to lightly beat the egg before adding it to the mixture. Add the dried herb mixture and mix with your hands, making sure you blend everything together well and scraping the side of the bowl with a cake spatula. This meatloaf mixture will be relatively wet, so if need be, add an additional ½ cup butter cracker crumbs.

- Fill a greased nonstick 9-inch/23-cm or 10-inch/25-cm pie pan with the meatloaf mixture and smooth the top with your hands or a cake spatula. Bake in the oven for approximately 20 to 30 minutes until partly cooked.

- While the meatloaf is baking, prepare the stuffing. Melt the butter in a frying pan and sauté the onion, celery, and carrots until softened. Remove from the heat and combine with the bread cubes and herbs in a bowl. Slowly add the chicken stock and mix with your hands to coat the bread cubes, adding more stock if necessary—the stuffing should be moist, but not soggy. Season with salt and pepper.

- Remove the pie from the oven and carefully place a layer of stuffing on the top of the partly cooked pie. Return to the oven and bake for an additional 10 to 15 minutes, or until the internal temperature reaches 165°F/74°C and the stuffing is lightly browned. Garnish the pie with dried cranberries, thyme sprigs, or dollops of Garlic Spuds (see page 126).

For the Meatloaf
½ tsp. dried thyme
½ tsp. dried oregano
½ tsp. dried basil
¼ tsp. cayenne pepper
¾ tsp. coarse sea salt
½ tsp. black pepper
1½ lb./680 g ground turkey
⅔ cup shredded carrot
½ cup finely diced yellow onion
¼ cup finely diced celery
¼ cup finely diced green bell pepper
¼ cup chopped fresh Italian parsley
1½ tbsp. minced garlic
1 cup butter cracker crumbs, plus an extra ½ cup if needed
⅓ cup finely grated Parmesan cheese
1 large egg, lightly beaten
¼ cup 2% milk
¼ cup ketchup
¼ cup tomato sauce
1 tsp. Worcestershire sauce
canola or vegetable oil spray, for greasing
dried cranberries, thyme sprigs, or Garlic Spuds (see page 126), for garnishing

For the Herbed Stuffing
3 tbsp. unsalted butter
½ cup finely diced yellow onion
¼ cup finely diced celery
¼ cup finely diced carrot
1¼ cups cubed fresh white bread (crusts removed)
1¼ cups cubed fresh 100% whole wheat bread (crusts removed), cubed
2 tbsp. chopped fresh Italian parsley
½ tsp. finely chopped fresh thyme leaves
½ tsp. dried rubbed sage
about ½ cup chicken stock, cooled
fine sea salt and black pepper, to taste

A LOAF IN EVERY POT (PIE)

Servings: 8

I adore chicken potpie any time of the year, so it seemed fitting that I create a meatloaf version. This recipe is special, because it takes everything that makes a chicken potpie so delicious and turns it into a soufflé-like meatloaf—light, flavorful, and reminiscent of the classic dish. Although I won't be giving up chicken potpies any time soon, I know this is a delectable alternative. And it can be made ahead of time and heated up just in time for guests.

TO MAKE

- First prepare the pastry dough. Place the flour and salt in a food processor. Add the butter and pulse a few times to mix. Add the vegetable shortening and pulse again until well mixed—the dough should be crumbly with pieces of visible butter. Add the water slowly while you pulse until the dough sticks together. Gather up the dough and flatten it on a lightly floured surface. Mold the dough into a ball, wrap in plastic wrap, and chill in the refrigerator for at least 30 minutes or up to 2 days before rolling. Short on time? I won't tell if you use frozen puff pastry. Just thaw the pastry as directed on the package and follow the recipe from there.

- For the meatloaf mixture, melt the butter in a frying pan and sauté the onion, carrot, and celery until softened. Set aside and cool. Combine the ground chicken with all the remaining meatloaf ingredients in a large bowl, add the cooled vegetables, and mix well with your hands. Divide the meatloaf mixture among 8 greased large (9 to 10-oz./250 to 280 g) ramekins. Fill to approximately ½ inch/1 cm from the rim. Keep the filled ramekins in the refrigerator, covered with plastic wrap, until you are ready to top them with the pastry dough.

- Preheat the oven to 375°F/190°C.

- On a lightly floured surface, roll out the chilled pastry dough to ¼ inch/5 mm thick. Using one of the ramekins as a guide, cut 8 circles from the dough about ½ inch/1 cm larger than the ramekin circumference. Lay a circle of dough over each meatloaf-filled ramekin. Crimp the edges using a fork or your fingers and brush with the egg wash (egg and milk mixture). Bake in the oven for 35 to 40 minutes, or until the crusts are golden brown and the internal temperature reaches 165°F/74°C. Let cool for 5 to 10 minutes, then serve.

For the Meatloaf
2 tbsp. unsalted butter
½ cup finely diced onion
½ cup finely diced carrot
¼ cup finely diced celery
2 lb./900 g ground chicken
1½ cups dry white bread crumbs
1 cup thawed and drained frozen petite peas
1 cup peeled and finely diced Yukon potatoes
½ cup low-sodium chicken stock
¼ cup heavy whipping cream
¼ cup dry sherry
2 tsp. canola oil
2 large eggs, lightly beaten
½ tsp. finely chopped fresh thyme leaves
½ tsp. poultry seasoning
1½ tsp. coarse kosher salt
½ tsp. black pepper
canola or vegetable oil spray, for greasing

For the Flaky Good Crust
3 cups all-purpose flour, plus extra for flouring
1 tsp. table salt
2 sticks (½ lb./225 g) unsalted butter, chilled and diced
½ cup vegetable shortening, chilled and diced
4–6 tbsp. cold water
2 egg yolks beaten with ¼ cup 2% milk, for glazing

WITH A TWIST

Inspired by beloved foods and world cuisines—modern twists on meatloaf are sure to become new classics in your kitchen. A Wing and a Prayer Loaf, My Thai Loaf, and Let's Salsa Loaf complete with dips and tips.

MAC 'N' BARB LOAF

Servings: 6 to 8

MACnificent Pasta buddies up with this hearty and delicious barbecue-inspired meatloaf. Loaded with cheese, a sweet and tangy barbecue sauce, bell peppers, and onions, it's topped with an unbeatable macaroni and cheese to make a tempting dream team.

TO MAKE

- Preheat the oven to 375°F/190°C.

- In a large bowl, combine all the meatloaf ingredients (except the topping) and mix well with your hands. (When it comes to the barbecue seasoning, I recommend using a basic variety instead of flavored ones, such as hickory or mesquite.)

- Fill a greased nonstick 9-inch/23-cm or 10-inch/25-cm pie pan with the meatloaf mixture. Smooth the top of the pie with your hands or a cake spatula and bake in the oven for approximately 20 to 30 minutes. Remove the pie from the oven and brush the top with extra barbecue sauce. (I use a sweet and tangy sauce, but you may use your favorite barbecue sauce; just note that it could change the overall flavor of the meatloaf, depending on the style of the sauce.) Return to the oven for an additional 5 minutes, or until the top of the meatloaf is glazed.

- While the meatloaf is baking, first prepare the pasta and cheese sauce for the MACnificient Pasta and then the crust topping, following the recipe on page 78.

- Remove the meatloaf again from the oven and carefully place a layer of the MACnificent Pasta about ½ inch/1 cm thick on the top of the partly cooked pie, then spread over a layer of the crust topping. (You will have some pasta mixture and topping left over, so bake the remainder in a separate, greased baking pan in the oven along with the meatloaf for 15 minutes until lightly browned, and serve as a side dish.) Return to the oven and bake for another 10 to 15 minutes, or until the internal temperature reaches 160°F/71°C and the pasta is lightly browned. Serve with the extra MACnificent Pasta, plus an extra helping of barbecue sauce on the side.

For the Meatloaf
- 1 lb. 4 oz./550 g ground chuck beef
- ¾ cup finely diced green bell pepper
- ¾ cup finely diced celery
- ¾ cup shredded carrot
- ½ cup finely diced yellow onion
- 2 tsp. minced garlic
- ⅔ cup shredded sharp yellow cheddar cheese
- ¼ cup plus 2 tbsp. sweet and tangy barbecue sauce, plus extra for glazing and serving
- ¼ cup plus 2 tbsp. ketchup
- 1 large egg, lightly beaten
- 1 cup dry white bread crumbs
- 1 tsp. barbecue seasoning
- ½ tsp. coarse sea salt
- ½ tsp. black pepper
- canola or vegetable oil spray, for greasing
- 1 batch MACnificient Pasta (see page 78), for topping

LET'S SALSA LOAF

Servings: 8 to 10

This peppy, multilayered meatloaf brings Mexican influences to a classic dish. I love how the middle layer of queso, hot peppers, and corn melts into the meatloaf, adding a richness and texture to each bite. Feel free to kick up the level of heat by adding more jalapeños or chili powder. Or you can use a hot and spicy salsa.

A chili-hot dish like this actually helps to cool you down. By creating heat in your mouth—the hotter the better—you'll break a sweat and lower your body temperature. Perfect food for a hot day? You bet!

TO MAKE

- Preheat the oven to 375°F/190°C.

- Combine the green bell pepper, onion, garlic, chili powder, oregano, cumin, salt, and pepper in a bowl. In a large bowl, combine the ground chuck beef, bread crumbs, eggs, and 1 cup of the salsa (reserve the remainder for glazing and serving). Add the green bell pepper mixture and mix well with your hands.

- In a food processor, lightly pulse the queso, corn, and cilantro with the red bell pepper and poblano and jalapeño peppers to mix.

- Grease two nonstick 10-inch x 5-inch/25-cm x 13-cm loaf pans (see note below). Divide the meatloaf mixture and cheese mixture in half. In the first pan, place approximately one-half of the divided meatloaf mixture in the loaf pan. Spread evenly into the corners. Spread the cheese mixture over this layer and top with a second layer of meatloaf. Smooth the surface of the meatloaf with a cake spatula. Repeat the process in the second loaf pan using the remaining meatloaf and cheese mixture. Bake in the oven for approximately 15 to 20 minutes.

- Remove the partly cooked meatloaves from the oven and brush with ¼ cup of the reserved salsa to glaze (this is optional). Return to the oven and bake for an additional 15 minutes, or until the internal temperature reaches 160°F/71°C. Remove from the oven and let cool for a few minutes.

- When cool enough to handle, carefully unmold the meatloaves. Slice and serve with the remaining salsa and the Sour Cream Lime Sauce (see page 153) on the side.

Note: The full recipe yields about 3 lb./1.3 kg meatloaf mixture and 1 lb./ 450 g cheese mixture. It's best to divide the recipe and bake in two 10-inch x 5-inch/25-cm x 13-cm loaf pans or a loaf pan that holds 4 lb./1.8 kg. You may freeze the second loaf and bake at a later date—a single loaf would feed 4 to 5 people. Be sure to increase your baking time if you are baking the meatloaf directly from the freezer.

For the Meatloaf

¾ cup finely diced green bell pepper
½ cup finely diced onion
2 tbsp. minced garlic
3 tbsp. chili powder
1 tsp. dried Mexican oregano
½ tsp. ground cumin
1 tsp. coarse kosher salt
½ tsp. black pepper
1½ lb./680 g ground chuck beef
1½ cups dry white bread crumbs
2 large eggs, lightly beaten
1½ cups medium hot salsa
2 cups shredded queso quesadilla
1 cup thawed and drained frozen or fresh corn kernels
2 tbsp. chopped fresh cilantro
¼ cup finely diced red bell pepper
2 tbsp. seeded and finely diced poblano pepper
2 tsp. seeded and finely diced jalapeño pepper
canola or vegetable oil spray, for greasing
Sour Cream Lime Sauce (see page 153), for serving

LOAF-A-ROMA

Servings: 6 to 8

Early on, when I was dabbling in my kitchen, I created an Italian-inspired meatloaf cake. After a few ingredient revisions, several tastings, and multiple sips of Chianti, I unveiled Loaf-A-Roma. Layered with angel hair pasta swirled in fresh marinara sauce, this cake soon became one of the store's most popular. It combines sweet Italian sausage, whole-milk mozzarella cheese, dry red wine, and fresh basil. What's not to like?

TO MAKE

- Preheat the oven to 375°F/190°C.

- In a bowl, combine the sun-dried tomatoes, onion, garlic, basil, mozzarella, oregano, salt, and pepper. In a large bowl, combine the ground chuck beef, Italian sausage, bread crumbs, tomato sauce, eggs, and red wine. Add the sun-dried tomato mixture and mix well with your hands. Instantly you'll smell the wonderful aroma of fresh basil, garlic, and Italian sausage. (I prefer sweet Italian sausage, but a spicier version would be just as tasty.)

- Grease two nonstick 8-inch/20-cm round cake pans. Fill each pan with about one-half of the meatloaf mixture. Smooth the tops with your hands or a cake spatula. Bake in the oven for approximately 20 to 30 minutes, or until the internal temperature reaches 160°F/71°C and the meatloaf tops are browned. Remove from the oven and cool for a few minutes.

- While the meatloaf layers are baking and cooling slightly, make the marinara sauce. In a stock pot or saucepan, heat the olive oil and sauté the onion, bell peppers, and celery over low heat for about 5 minutes. Add the red wine and cook until almost dry. Add the crushed tomatoes, oregano, basil, and garlic and bring to a simmer. Cover and simmer for 20 minutes, stirring frequently. Blend with an immersion blender until smooth. Season with salt, pepper, and sugar (the sugar helps round out the acid from the tomatoes and brings out the flavors).

- Cook the pasta according to the package instructions until al dente. (I like angel hair, but any long, thin pasta will work.) Drain thoroughly and toss with as much marinara sauce as you like.

- When cool enough to handle, unmold the meatloaf layers carefully. Place one Loaf-A-Roma layer on a nonstick sheet pan or cookie sheet. Cover it with a layer of the pasta and marinara mixture. Top this with the second meatloaf layer and finish with a final layer of pasta/marinara. Sprinkle with Parmesan and season with an Italian herb blend. You may also add extra marinara in between the layers, depending upon how much sauce you prefer. Let cool completely, then cover and refrigerate until ready to serve. Reheat according to the instructions on page 14. Garnish the hot meatloaf with fresh basil leaves and, of course, serve with any remaining steaming marinara on the side.

For the Meatloaf

½ cup drained and chopped sun-dried tomatoes in oil
⅓ cup finely diced yellow onion
1½ tbsp. minced garlic
1 cup chopped fresh basil, plus extra leaves for garnishing
8 oz./225 g fresh whole-milk mozzarella cheese, cut into small cubes
1¾ tsp. dried oregano
1 tsp. coarse sea salt
½ tsp. black pepper
1 lb./450 g ground chuck beef
8 oz./225 g skinless sweet Italian sausage
1 cup dry white bread crumbs
½ cup tomato sauce
2 large eggs, lightly beaten
¼ cup dry red wine
canola or vegetable oil spray
1 lb./450 g dry angel hair pasta, or any long, thin pasta
grated Parmesan cheese, to taste
dried Italian herb blend, to taste

For the Marinara Sauce

2 tbsp. extra virgin olive oil
½ cup finely diced yellow onion
¼ cup finely diced red bell pepper
¼ cup finely diced green bell pepper
¼ cup finely diced celery
¼ cup dry red wine
1 (28-oz./800-g) can crushed tomatoes
2 tsp. dried oregano
2 tsp. dried basil
1 tbsp. minced garlic
½ tsp. red pepper flakes (optional)
coarse sea salt and black pepper, to taste
granulated sugar, to taste

MY THAI LOAF

Servings: 6 to 8

Thai-riffic herbs, such as fresh ginger, basil, and cilantro, a touch of chili garlic paste, lime juice, and shallots give new life to simple ground beef. This innovative twist on a Thai beef salad topped with delicious peanut sauce and cilantro rice is definitely a showstopper.

TO MAKE

- Preheat the oven to 375°F/190°C.

- In a bowl, combine the shallots, cilantro, basil, mint, garlic, ginger, Serrano pepper, curry powder, red pepper flakes, salt, and pepper. Add the lime juice, sesame oil, fish sauce, and chili garlic paste and mix well.

- In a large bowl, combine the ground chuck beef, bread crumbs, and eggs. Add the herb-and-spice mixture and mix well with your hands. Take a moment to enjoy the aroma of this delicious combination of Thai-based flavors.

- Divide the meatloaf mixture into 6 portions and place in a greased large nonstick 6-cup cupcake/muffin pan. Round the top of each meatloaf cupcake with your hands to form a dome. Bake in the oven for 30 minutes, or until internal temperature reaches 160°F/71°C and the cupcake tops are browned. (If you have extra meatloaf mixture, put the remainder in a greased loaf pan and bake in the same way as the cupcakes.) Remove from the oven and let cool for a few minutes.

- While the meatloaf cupcakes are baking and cooling slightly, prepare the cilantro coconut rice. Cook the rice according to the package instructions. Add the cilantro and as much or as little coconut milk as you'd like. (The coconut milk helps the rice hold its shape when scooped onto the cupcakes, but you can omit the milk and simply serve the rice as a side dish.) Season with salt and mix lightly, being careful not to mush the rice.

- For the peanut lime sauce, whisk together all the ingredients in a small bowl with a fork or wire whisk. Blend with an immersion blender or in a food processor to thin slightly. If you want to serve the sauce on the side as well, make a double batch. (Alternatively, the sauce can be made ahead of time and then covered with plastic wrap and stored in the refrigerator. Bring back to room temperature before using or serving.)

- Unmold the meatloaf cupcakes carefully and set on paper towels to absorb any extra moisture. Spread a thin layer of the peanut lime sauce onto the tops of the cupcakes. Scoop the cilantro coconut rice on top of each cupcake—try using an ice-cream scoop for this. Garnish with crushed peanuts. Serve with the remaining rice on the side, and the extra sauce if you've made some.

For the Meatloaf
¾ cup finely diced shallots
½ cup chopped fresh cilantro
¼ cup plus 1 tbsp. chopped fresh basil
2 tbsp. plus 1 tsp. chopped fresh mint
2 tbsp. minced garlic
2 tbsp. chopped fresh ginger
1 tbsp. plus 1 tsp. seeded and chopped Serrano pepper
¼ tsp. lemongrass curry powder
¼ tsp. red pepper flakes
1 tsp. coarse sea salt
¼ tsp. black pepper
½ cup strained fresh lime juice
1 tbsp. sesame oil
1 tbsp. Thai fish sauce
1 tsp. Thai chili garlic paste
1½ lb./680 g ground chuck beef
1½ cups panko bread crumbs
2 large eggs, lightly beaten
crushed roasted peanuts, for garnishing
canola or vegetable oil spray, for greasing

For the Cilantro Coconut Rice
about 3 cups long-grain white rice (to yield 6 cups cooked)
¼ cup chopped fresh cilantro
about 5–6 tbsp. coconut milk (optional)
fine sea salt, to taste

For the Peanut Lime Sauce
½ cup unsweetened natural peanut butter
½ cup water
2 tbsp. strained fresh lime juice
1 tbsp. low-sodium soy sauce
1 tbsp. packed light brown sugar
1 tsp. minced fresh ginger
1 tsp. minced garlic
¼ tsp. red pepper flakes

EL LOAFO DEL FUEGO

Servings: 6

El Loafo del Fuego (the loaf of fire, or something like that . . .) was so much fun to create. My nephew John and I were in my kitchen dreaming up some of my initial recipes. "Let's try pork, almonds, and green olives. And then we'll toss in spicy chorizo, hot peppers, onions, and sherry." A few more ingredients and we'd created one of our most complex and innovative recipes.

For the Meatloaf

1 batch Garlic Spuds (see page 126), for topping
2 tbsp. unsalted butter
½ cup plus 2 tbsp. finely diced yellow bell pepper
½ cup plus 2 tbsp. finely diced red bell pepper
¼ cup minced jalapeño peppers (seed to minimize heat), plus extra, sliced, for garnishing
2 tbsp. minced Serrano peppers (seed to minimize heat), plus extra, sliced, for garnishing
½ cup finely diced yellow onion
2 tbsp. minced garlic
1½ lb./680 g ground pork
8 oz./225 g hot chorizo, skinned and crumbled
⅓ cup ground almonds (almond meal)
¼ cup drained and finely diced green olives stuffed with pimento
1 cup dry white bread crumbs
2 large eggs, lightly beaten
¼ cup dry sherry
½ tsp. coarse sea salt
½ tsp. black pepper
canola or vegetable oil spray, for greasing
paprika, for garnishing
Sherry Mushroom Sauce (see page 151), for serving

TO MAKE

- First roast and then mash the garlic for the Garlic Spuds, following the recipe on page 126. Reduce the oven to 375°F/190°C.

- Melt the butter in a frying pan and sauté all the bell peppers and hot peppers, onion, and garlic until softened. Set aside and cool.

- Combine the cooled vegetables and all the remaining meatloaf ingredients in a bowl. Mix well with your hands—be sure to blend together everything, scraping the side of the bowl with a spatula.

- Divide the meatloaf mixture into 6 portions and place in a lightly greased, large nonstick 6-cup cupcake/muffin pan. Round the top of each meatloaf cupcake with your hands to form a dome. Bake in the oven for approximately 30 to 40 minutes, or until the internal temperature reaches 160°F/71°C and the cupcake tops are browned. Remove from the oven and let cool for a few minutes.

- While the meatloaf cupcakes are baking and cooling slightly, finish preparing the Garlic Spuds according to the recipe on page 126.

- When cool enough to handle, unmold the meatloaf cupcakes carefully and set on a flat surface in preparation for "frosting." Insert any pastry tip into a 12 to 14-inch/30 to 35-cm pastry bag and fill with the hot Garlic Spuds (use caution, because the bag can be hot to the touch). Have fun and be creative with your designs. Garnish with a light dusting of paprika and a slice of jalapeño or Serrano pepper. If you'd like the potatoes to be golden brown, place the "frosted" cupcakes under a hot broiler for a few minutes. Serve with Sherry Mushroom Sauce (see page 151).

The ground almonds give this meatloaf a very distinctive texture—it's smoother than most but stays moist and succulent, almost like a pâté. And the olives and chorizo give the finished loaf a distinctly Hispanic twist. If you want a picnic dish, this one's particularly good eaten cold, too.

PARTY HEARTY PIZZA LOAF

Servings: about 12 (6 per Stromboli)

Everyone knows pizza comes in many flavors, shapes, and sizes. So how about a meatloaf-style pizza? Chock-full of mushrooms, pepperoni, Italian sausage, and green bell peppers, it's clearly supreme and a great addition to any party. It's got a little heat, so if you like, cut back on the red pepper flakes and pepperoni. Roll it like a Stromboli and enjoy with Cynthia's Salad or a tangy Caesar salad.

TO MAKE

- Preheat the oven to 350°F/180°C.

- In a small bowl, combine the Parmesan, garlic, oregano, and red pepper flakes. In a large bowl, gently mix together the Italian sausage and ground chuck beef. (I prefer to use a mild Italian sausage, but if you like spicy, go ahead.) Add all the remaining meatloaf ingredients and the Parmesan mixture. Mix well with your hands and set aside.

- Cover a sheet pan or cookie sheet with parchment paper and lightly grease with extra virgin olive oil. Place one package of prepared pizza dough on the prepared pan. Gently stretch (or roll) the dough into a rectangle approximately 12 inches x 9 inches/30 cm x 23 cm. Spread one-half of the meatloaf mixture on top of the dough, leaving a 1-inch/2.5-cm border on each side. (You can also spread a thin layer of pizza sauce onto the dough before adding the meatloaf mixture, if you prefer more sauce.)

- Roll up the dough around the filling to form a log, then seal the seam by pinching lightly. Fold in the two ends to secure the filling. Trim the excess dough and turn the Stromboli seam-side down. Flatten the log and make diagonal cuts across it, 1½ inches/4 cm apart, along its length. Repeat with the second package of pizza dough and meatloaf mixture. Brush the logs with a little extra virgin olive oil, and sprinkle with kosher salt, if you like.

- Bake in the oven for 10 to 15 minutes. Turn the logs over and bake for an additional 10 minutes, or until the internal temperature reaches 160°F/71°C and the dough is golden brown. Cool slightly, then slice and serve with extra pizza sauce, of course!

For the Meatloaf

2 tbsp. grated Parmesan cheese
1 tbsp. minced garlic
½ tsp. dried oregano
⅛ tsp. red pepper flakes
10 oz./280 g skinless sweet
   Italian sausage
6 oz./175 g ground chuck beef
½ cup chopped white mushrooms
¼ cup finely diced green bell pepper
¼ cup finely diced onion
½ cup diced mozzarella cheese
¼ cup diced pepperoni
¾ cup dry white bread crumbs
¾ cup pizza sauce, plus extra for
   spreading (optional) and serving
1 large egg, lightly beaten

For the Pizza Dough Wrapping

2 (13–14-oz./375–400 g) packages
   refrigerated prepared thick-crust
   pizza dough (or make your own)
extra virgin olive oil, for greasing
   and brushing
kosher salt (optional)

You'll find Italian sausage or "salsiccia" labeled either "hot" or "sweet" at the grocery store (sometimes it's offered with additional seasonings—slightly licorice-tasting fennel is a common extra—too). I've specified the sweet type here, but you can switch to hot if you'd like to turn up the piquancy level.

KICKIN' CAJUN LOAF

Servings: 6

Spicy and nice, this is. Topped with Garlic Spuds, this Cajun-inspired meatloaf tickles the taste buds of spice lovers everywhere. Really want some heat? Kick it up even more!

TO MAKE

- First roast and then mash the garlic for the Garlic Spuds, following the recipe on page 126. Reduce the oven to 375°F/190°C.

- Combine the butter, bell peppers, onion, celery, and Worcestershire and Tabasco sauces in a saucepan and cook until the liquid has evaporated. Add the ketchup and cream, and then stir lightly to blend. Set aside and let cool.

- In a large bowl, combine the ground chuck beef, pork, bread crumbs, eggs, cayenne, salt, and pepper—if you crave more heat, just increase the amount of cayenne pepper and toss in a little minced jalapeño pepper. Add the cooled bell pepper mixture and mix well with your hands.

- Divide the meatloaf mixture into 6 portions and place in a lightly greased, large nonstick 6-cup cupcake/muffin pan. Round the top of each meatloaf cupcake with your hands to form a dome. Bake in the oven for approximately 30 to 40 minutes, or until the internal temperature reaches 160°F/71°C and the cupcake tops are browned. Remove from the oven and let cool for a few minutes.

- While the meatloaf cupcakes are baking and cooling slightly, finish preparing the Garlic Spuds, following the recipe on page 126.

- When cool enough to handle, unmold the meatloaf cupcakes carefully and set on a flat surface in preparation for "frosting." Using a small cake spatula, spread the hot Garlic Spuds onto each cupcake and then shape creatively—I like square tops, rounded tops, and even pointy tops. But if time doesn't permit, simply scoop the spuds on top of each Kickin' Cajun cupcake. Finish each with a sprinkling of finely diced red and green bell peppers. If you'd like the potatoes to be golden brown, place the "frosted" cupcakes under a hot broiler for a few minutes. Serve with Sherry Mushroom Sauce (see page 151).

For the Meatloaf

1 batch Garlic Spuds (see page 126), for topping
2 tbsp. unsalted butter
¼ cup finely diced green bell pepper, plus extra for topping
¼ cup finely diced red bell pepper, plus extra for topping
⅔ cup finely diced yellow onion
¼ cup finely diced celery
3 tbsp. Worcestershire sauce
3 tbsp. Tabasco sauce
½ cup ketchup
½ cup heavy cream
1½ lb./680 g ground chuck beef
8 oz./225 g ground pork
1 cup dry white bread crumbs
2 large eggs, lightly beaten
1 tsp. cayenne pepper, or to taste
2 tsp. coarse sea salt
½ tsp. black pepper
minced jalapeño pepper, to taste (optional)
canola or vegetable oil spray, for greasing
Sherry Mushroom Sauce (see page 151), for serving

A WING AND A PRAYER LOAF

Servings: 6

Buffalo wings are definitely favorites among game watchers, partygoers, and chicken lovers. But everyone knows they can be messy to eat. So I set out to capture the flavor of hot wings in a tidy, easy-to-eat package. I created this recipe on a whim, and to my surprise and joy, it's been heralded in top magazines as a favorite thing to eat. "You're just going to have to try it to understand its genius," says Time Out Chicago.

For the Meatloaf
2 lb./900 g ground chicken
1¼ cups finely diced celery
1 cup finely diced yellow onion
1 cup shredded yellow cheddar cheese
1½ cups crumbled blue cheese
4 tbsp. butter, softened
¼ cup hot wing sauce
2 tbsp. mayonnaise
2 large eggs, lightly beaten
1 cup panko bread crumbs
2 tsp. paprika
2 tsp. poultry seasoning
1 tsp. coarse sea salt
1 tsp. black pepper
canola or vegetable oil spray,
    for greasing

For the Blue Cheese Crumb Topping
¼ cup unsalted butter, chilled
½ cup crumbled blue cheese
1 cup panko bread crumbs
1 tbsp. finely chopped fresh chives

For the Ranch Dressing
1 cup mayonnaise
½ cup unsweetened plain yogurt
¼ cup buttermilk
1 tbsp. finely chopped fresh chives
1 garlic clove, crushed
½ tsp. Tabasco sauce
fine sea salt and black pepper, to taste

TO MAKE

- Preheat the oven to 375°F/190°C.

- Combine all the ingredients in a bowl and mix well with your hands—be sure to blend everything together, scraping the side of the bowl with a cake spatula. (If you like your "wings" spicier, you can increase the amount of hot sauce, but you'll also have to up the quantity of bread crumbs to maintain the correct consistency.)

- Place the meatloaf mixture in a greased nonstick 10-inch x 5-inch/25-cm x 13-cm loaf pan. Bake in the oven for approximately 45 minutes, or until the internal temperature reaches 165°F/74°C and the top is golden brown. Remove from the oven and let cool for a few minutes.

- While the meatloaf is baking and cooling slightly, prepare the blue cheese crumb topping. Cut the butter into small pieces. Combine with the blue cheese and bread crumbs in a bowl and mix well with your hands. Set aside.

- When cool enough to handle, carefully unmold the meatloaf and set on paper towels to absorb any excess moisture. Then transfer from the paper towels to a cookie sheet and set aside. Using a rolling pin, roll out a layer of the blue cheese crumb topping to fit the top of the meatloaf. Pat on gently and sprinkle with the chives. Let cool completely, then cover and refrigerate until ready to serve. Reheat according to the instructions on page 14. In the meantime, whisk together all the ingredients for the ranch dressing with a wire whisk, seasoning with salt and pepper. Slice and serve the hot meatloaf immediately with the tangy ranch dressing.

HOLY MOLY CHICKEN FRIJOLE

Servings: 6 to 8

Fresh and flavorful, this creation is loaded with colorful ingredients, such as bell peppers, corn, cilantro, and red onion. Add tender ground chicken and spices, top with fajita-style peppers, and you've got an ideal spring and summer meatloaf.

TO MAKE

- In a large frying pan, heat the canola oil and sauté the corn, beans, red onion, bell peppers, garlic, fine sea salt, and ⅛ teaspoon black pepper until softened. Set aside and let cool.

- Preheat the oven to 375°F/190°C.

- In a large bowl, combine all the remaining meatloaf ingredients, including another ½ teaspoon black pepper. Add the cooled corn-and-bean mixture and mix well with your hands.

- Fill a greased nonstick 9-inch/23-cm or 10-inch/25-cm pie pan with the meatloaf mixture. Smooth the top of the pie with your hands or a cake spatula and bake in the oven for approximately 20 to 30 minutes.

- While the meatloaf is baking, prepare the fajita peppers. Heat the canola oil in a frying pan and sauté the onion and bell peppers, seasoning with salt and pepper, until softened—avoid overcooking to retain the bright colors. Drain on paper towels and let cool.

- Remove the pie from the oven and carefully spread a thin layer, about ⅛ inch/4 mm thick, of the mashed black beans followed by a layer of fajita peppers on the top of the partly cooked pie. Return to the oven and bake for an additional 10 to 15 minutes, or until the internal temperature reaches 165°F/74°C. Serve with cool and refreshing Sour Cream Lime Sauce (see page 153).

For the Meatloaf

1 tbsp. canola oil
½ cup thawed and drained frozen corn kernels
½ cup rinsed and drained canned black beans
½ cup finely diced red onion
⅓ cup finely diced red bell pepper
⅓ cup finely diced yellow bell pepper
⅓ cup finely diced green bell pepper
1 tbsp. minced garlic
⅛ tsp. fine sea salt
½ tsp. plus ⅛ tsp. black pepper
1½ lb./680 g ground chicken
2 cups panko bread crumbs
¾ cup drained canned petite diced tomatoes
¼ cup chopped fresh cilantro
1 large egg, lightly beaten
⅓ cup strained fresh lime juice
3 tbsp. sour cream
1½ tsp. coarse sea salt
1 tsp. ground cumin
½ tsp. paprika
¼ tsp. garlic powder
¼ tsp. onion powder
¼ tsp. cayenne pepper
¼ tsp. chili powder
canola or vegetable oil spray, for greasing
Sour Cream Lime Sauce (see page 153), for serving

For the Fajita Peppers

2 tbsp. canola oil
1 cup thinly sliced yellow onion
¾ cup thinly sliced green bell pepper
¾ cup thinly sliced red bell pepper
¾ cup thinly sliced yellow bell pepper
fine sea salt and black pepper, to taste
1½ cups drained and mashed canned black beans

SASSY TURKEY SAUSAGE

Servings: 6

This zippy blend of turkey, spicy turkey sausage, and fragrant herbs and spices gives this recipe a primo place at the dinner table. Topped with Whipped Sweet Potatoes and marshmallows, it raises turkey to a new level.

TO MAKE

- Preheat the oven to 375°F/190°C.

- First bake the sweet potatoes for the Whipped Sweet Potatoes, following the recipe on page 130.

- While the sweet potatoes are baking, prepare the meatloaf mixture. In a bowl, combine the onion, celery, bell pepper, garlic, and tomato, Worcestershire, and Tabasco sauces, mixing until the vegetables are well coated. Add the ketchup and stir lightly to blend.

- In a large bowl, combine all the remaining meatloaf ingredients. Add the prepared vegetable mixture to the bowl and mix well with your hands.

- Divide the meatloaf mixture into 6 portions and place in a lightly greased regular nonstick 6-cup cupcake/muffin pan. Round the top of each meatloaf cupcake with your hands to form a dome. Bake in the oven for approximately 30 to 40 minutes, or until the internal temperature reaches 165°F/74°C and the cupcake tops are golden brown. Remove from the oven and let cool for a few minutes.

- While the meatloaf cupcakes are baking and cooling slightly, finish preparing the Whipped Sweet Potatoes, following the recipe on page 130.

- When cool enough to handle, carefully unmold the meatloaf cupcakes and top with the hot Whipped Sweet Potatoes. Garnish each cupcake with 3 mini marshmallows (or more if you have a sweet tooth!), and enjoy with Cranberry Sauce (see page 154).

For the Meatloaf
1 batch Whipped Sweet Potatoes
  (see page 130), for topping
1 cup finely diced yellow onion
½ cup finely diced celery
¼ cup finely diced red bell pepper
1½ tbsp. minced garlic
⅓ cup tomato sauce
1 tsp. Worcestershire sauce
1 tsp. Tabasco sauce
⅓ cup ketchup
1 lb./450 g ground turkey
8 oz./225 g skinless spicy Italian turkey
  sausage, crumbled
1 cup butter cracker crumbs
2 large eggs, lightly beaten
½ cup chopped fresh curly or
  Italian parsley
½ tsp. finely chopped fresh
  thyme leaves
½ tsp. dried oregano
½ tsp. dried basil
½ tsp. dried marjoram
¼ tsp. cayenne pepper
2 tsp. coarse sea salt
½ tsp. black pepper
canola or vegetable oil spray,
  for greasing
mini marshmallows, for garnishing
Cranberry Sauce (see page 154),
  for serving

MEATLESS LOAVES

Savory and rewarding recipes created from grains, veggies, and seafood, such as Omega-3 Loaf. Rootin' for Barley or looking for something Falafel-ly Good? There's a meatless loaf for every appetite.

MACNIFICENT PASTA

Servings: 6

I'm very particular about macaroni and cheese. I didn't
care for it growing up, but I know everyone likes a
big helping of this classic comfort food. So I created
a recipe that even I would adore. Now I can't get
enough of MACnificent Pasta—a sophisticated take on
this favorite dish. It's rich, and very MACnificent!

TO MAKE

- In a large saucepan, cook the pasta according to the package instructions until al dente. Drain thoroughly. Toss with a little vegetable oil to keep the shells from sticking together, if not using immediately. Set aside.

- Preheat the oven to 375°F/190°C.

- In a saucepan, melt the butter and gradually add the flour, stirring until smooth. Whisk in the milk and cream with a wire whisk and bring to a boil, stirring constantly. Continue to cook, stirring, until the sauce thickens. Reduce the heat to low and add all the cheeses. Whisk until smooth. (You'll get a workout with this step, because the cheese blend is thick.) Whisk in the parsley, spices, and seasonings, and then remove from heat.

- Toss the cooked pasta with the cheese sauce until well blended. Divide the pasta mixture into 6 portions and place in a lightly greased large nonstick 6-cup cupcake/muffin pan. If you have some left over, place it in a separate greased nonstick baking pan for baking alongside the cupcakes.

- In a bowl, combine all ingredients for the crumb topping, mixing well. Spread a layer of the topping over each pasta cupcake. Bake in the oven for approximately 15 minutes, or until the cupcake tops are golden brown. Remove from the oven and let cool for a few minutes, then unmold carefully when cool enough to handle.

For the Pasta
2 cups dry small pasta shells
vegetable oil, for tossing with the pasta (optional)
4 tbsp. unsalted butter
¼ cup all-purpose flour
1 cup 2% milk
¼ cup heavy cream
2⅔ cups shredded sharp yellow cheddar cheese
1⅓ cups shredded sharp white cheddar cheese
⅔ cup shredded Monterey Jack cheese
½ cup grated Parmesan cheese
¼ cup chopped fresh curly parsley
½ tsp. dry mustard
¼ tsp. cayenne pepper
1 tbsp. coarse sea salt
¼ tsp. black pepper
canola and vegetable oil spray, for greasing

For the Crumb Topping
½ cup panko bread crumbs
⅓ cup shredded sharp yellow cheddar cheese
2 tbsp. grated Parmesan cheese
1 tbsp. unsalted butter, softened

Panko bread crumbs, used to top these little cupcakes, originated in Japan and are lighter and crispier than regular crumbs. Although the regular type will work fine, if you can find the panko variety they'll add an extra-delectable crunch to your creations.

NUTTY VEGGIE LOAF

Servings: 6

This is one of my favorite nonmeat recipes. I love it because it's loaded with luscious nuts, carrots, and bell peppers. It's savory with a touch of sweetness and has a wonderful texture—almost like zucchini bread. Not to mention, it's very pretty when you decorate it with thin slices of zucchini, yellow squash, and plum tomatoes. Try it with Cranberry Sauce or Red Pepper Coulis.

Packed full of antioxidants, including vitamin E, plus a wide range of other vitamins and minerals, walnuts, pecans, and sunflower kernels are great additions to your diet. So, as well as tasting good, this loaf is a great pick if you want to eat healthily, too.

TO MAKE

- Preheat the oven to 375°F/190°C.

- In a frying pan, melt the butter and sauté the mushrooms, onion, and bell peppers until softened. Add the garlic and cook over low heat until the mixture is almost dry. Set aside and cool for a few minutes. While the vegetables are cooling, combine all the remaining loaf ingredients except the eggs and bread crumbs in a large bowl. Then add the cooled vegetables, eggs, and bread crumbs, and mix well with your hands.

- Place the loaf mixture in a greased nonstick 10-inch x 5-inch/ 25-cm x 13-cm loaf pan and smooth the top with your hands or a cake spatula. Bake in the oven for approximately 45 to 50 minutes, or until the internal temperature reaches 160°F/71°C and the top is browned. Remove from the oven and let cool for a few minutes.

- While the loaf is baking and cooling slightly, prepare the vegetables for the topping. In a bowl, toss the zucchini and yellow squash with olive oil to lightly coat. Sprinkle with salt and pepper. Spread out in a single layer on a nonstick cookie sheet. Bake in the oven with the loaf for approximately 15 to 20 minutes until just softened and slightly browned. Gently remove the vegetable slices from the pan, set aside, and wait for the tomatoes!

- In another bowl (or the same one you used for the squash), gently coat the tomato slices with olive oil. Spread in a single layer on the cookie sheet or roasting pan and bake for approximately 15 minutes until just softened and slightly browned. Gently remove the tomato slices from the pan.

- When cool enough to handle, carefully unmold the loaf and spread a thin layer of ketchup or Cranberry Sauce (see page 154) over the top. Place the roasted slices of zucchini, yellow squash, and tomatoes in a decorative pattern on top of the loaf. Serve immediately with a heaping dish of sweet and tangy Cranberry Sauce or Red Pepper Coulis (see page 155).

For the Meatloaf

2 tbsp. unsalted butter
1½ cups chopped white mushrooms
1¼ cups finely diced yellow onion
⅓ cup finely diced green bell pepper
⅓ cup finely diced yellow bell pepper
2 tsp. minced garlic
4 cups shredded carrots
scant 2 cups finely diced celery
¼ cup chopped fresh Italian parsley
⅓ cup chopped walnuts
⅓ cup chopped pecans
⅓ cup unsalted sunflower kernels
1 tsp. coarse sea salt
½ tsp. black pepper
½ tsp. dried basil
1 tsp. dried oregano
½ tsp. dried marjoram
½ tsp. paprika
¼ cup finely grated Parmesan cheese
¼ cup ketchup, plus extra for topping
   (optional)
4 large eggs, lightly beaten
4½ cups coarse fresh whole wheat
   bread crumbs
canola or vegetable oil spray,
   for greasing
Cranberry Sauce (see page 154),
   for topping and serving (optional),
   or Red Pepper Coulis (see page 155),
   for serving

For the Nutty Veggie Topping

½ zucchini, thinly sliced
½ yellow squash, thinly sliced
3 oz./85 g (¾ cup) thinly sliced
   plum tomatoes
extra virgin olive oil, for coating
coarse sea salt and black pepper,
   to taste

ROOTIN' FOR BARLEY LOAF

Servings: 6

Creating this recipe was a delightful kitchen experience. I combined every root vegetable I like, added the requisite garlic, onions, and red wine, plus more favorites such as barley and crimini mushrooms. I sautéed a little here, mixed a little there—and presto, a sweet, savory, and delicious vegetarian loaf was born. Topped with a dollop of sour cream or crème fraîche and a medley of roasted beets and carrots, it's absolutely fabulous.

TO MAKE

- Preheat the oven to 375°F/190°C.

- In a large frying pan, melt the butter and sauté the squash, parsnip, carrot, turnip, onion, and garlic until lightly softened. Add the red wine, salt, and pepper, and then simmer until the liquid has evaporated. Set aside and cool.

- In a bowl, combine the mushrooms, cooked barley, uncooked oats, eggs, mustard, and herbs. Add to the cooled vegetables and mix lightly.

- Divide the loaf mixture into 6 portions and place in lightly greased, large nonstick 6-cup cupcake/muffin pan. Round the top of each meatloaf cupcake with your hands to form a dome. Bake in the oven for approximately 30 minutes, or until the internal temperature reaches 160°F/71°C and the cupcakes are browned. Remove from the oven and cool for a few minutes.

- While the cupcakes are baking, prepare the vegetable topping. Peel the beets and cut into ⅛-inch/3-mm thick slices, then place in a bowl. Peel the carrots and cut diagonally into slices the same thickness as the beets. (You can use a knife or a mandolin for this.) Place in a separate bowl. Add half the canola oil (¼ cup) to each bowl and toss to coat. Spread the vegetables in a single layer on a nonstick sheet pan or cookie sheet and sprinkle with salt and pepper. Roast in the oven along with the cupcakes for approximately 15 to 20 minutes, or until tender. Remove from the oven and let cool slightly.

- When cool enough to handle, unmold the cupcakes carefully and spread a thin layer of sour cream or crème fraîche on top of each. (Either of these adds brightness to this sweet and earthy vegetable barley creation.) Layer the roasted beets and carrots alternately in a shingle pattern or another decorative way. Enjoy with an extra dollop of sour cream or crème fraîche.

For the Meatloaf

4 tbsp. unsalted butter
1½ cups finely diced butternut squash
1 cup grated parsnip
½ cup finely diced carrot
½ cup finely diced turnip
½ cup finely diced onion
1½ tbsp. minced garlic
½ cup dry red wine
1 tsp. coarse kosher salt
¼ tsp. black pepper
2 cups chopped crimini mushrooms
1 cup cooked barley
1 cup 100% whole grain rolled oats (uncooked)
2 large eggs, lightly beaten
2 tsp. Dijon mustard
½ tsp. dried oregano
1 tbsp. finely chopped fresh thyme leaves
canola or vegetable oil spray, for greasing
1 cup sour cream or crème fraîche for topping, plus extra for serving

For the Roasted Beet and Carrot Topping

2 whole beets
3 carrots
about ½ cup canola oil
fine sea salt and black pepper, to taste

YENTL LENTL LOAF

Servings: 6 to 8

Even meat lovers rave about this very special vegetarian and gluten-free recipe. Loaded with lentils, brown rice, mushrooms, and mozzarella cheese, it's hearty and healthy. Enjoy it hot with Red Pepper Coulis or as a cold sandwich in your favorite wrap.

TO MAKE

- First prepare the Red Pepper Coulis, following the recipe on page 155. Set aside enough of the coulis to spread a thin covering over the layers, then cover and chill the remainder in the refrigerator for serving on the side.

- Preheat the oven to 375°F/190°C.

- Measure and set aside the various ingredients for this recipe. While there are only a few steps to perfection, following them will be useful. Place the lentils in a saucepan and cover with cold water. Bring to a rolling boil and cook for a few minutes, then drain and return the lentils to the pan. Cover with the lid and set aside to let the cooking process continue while you prepare the rice—the lentils should be tender.

- Next, place the rice, V8 vegetable juice, and water in a large saucepan. Cover and simmer over low heat for about 10 minutes, or until most of the liquid has been absorbed. Add the lentils and continue cooking over low heat, stirring occasionally, until all the liquid has been absorbed. Remove from the heat.

- In a dry, nonstick frying pan, sauté the mushrooms over medium heat until all the liquid has evaporated. Add the carrot, onion, and celery, and then sauté for an additional 2 minutes. Add the vegetables to the rice-and-lentil mixture.

- In a bowl, combine the roasted red bell pepper puree, mozzarella, Parmesan, eggs, basil, salt, and pepper. Add this to the rice-and-lentil mixture and mix well with a wooden spoon until the cheese has melted.

For the Meatloaf

1 batch Red Pepper Coulis (see page 155), for spreading and serving
¾ cup brown lentils
1 cup brown long-grain rice
2 cups V8 vegetable juice
1 cup water
3 cups thinly sliced white mushrooms
¾ cup shredded carrot
½ cup finely diced yellow onion
½ cup finely diced celery
⅓ cup drained and pureed roasted red bell peppers from a jar
8 oz./225 g low-moisture part-skim mozzarella cheese, cubed
½ cup finely grated Parmesan cheese
2 large eggs, lightly beaten
2 tbsp. finely chopped fresh basil
½ tsp. coarse sea salt
½ tsp. black pepper
canola or vegetable oil spray, for greasing

For the Mélange of Julienned Bell Peppers

2 tbsp. canola or olive oil
¾ cup finely julienned green bell pepper
¾ cup finely julienned red bell pepper
¾ cup finely julienned orange bell pepper
¾ cup finely julienned yellow bell pepper
coarse sea salt and black pepper, to taste

- Grease two nonstick 8-inch/20-cm round cake pans. Fill each pan with about one-half of the loaf mixture. Smooth the tops with your hands or a cake spatula. Bake in the oven for approximately 20 to 30 minutes, or until the internal temperature reaches 160°F/71°C and the loaf tops are browned. Remove from the oven and let cool for a few minutes.

- While the loaf layers are baking and cooling slightly, prepare the julienned bell peppers. Heat the oil in a frying pan. Add all the bell peppers and sauté for about 10 to 15 minutes until softened—avoid overcooking to retain their bright colors. Season with salt and pepper.

- When cool enough to handle, unmold the loaf layers carefully. Spread a thin layer of the reserved Red Pepper Coulis over the first layer of Yentl Lentl. Spread over a layer of the sautéed bell peppers and place the second layer of the loaf over this. Decorate the top of the cake with a thin layer of Red Pepper Coulis and the remaining sautéed bell peppers. Serve immediately with the chilled Red Pepper Coulis.

THE FALAFEL-LY GOOD LOAF

Servings: 6

Falafel is such a popular dish in Mediterranean cuisine that it seemed the perfect choice for The Meatloaf Bakery, given my Lebanese heritage. Filling and flavorful, this loaf packs in those wonderful falafel spices and tastes even more delicious with a heaping helping of freshly made Tabouleh, along with tahini sauce or hummus.

TO MAKE

- Preheat the oven to 375°F/190°C.

- In a small bowl, soak the bulgur wheat in the water for about 15 minutes until softened. Squeeze out any excess water and then transfer the bulgur wheat to a larger bowl.

- Lightly pulse the garbanzo beans in a food processor until coarsely mashed and add to the bowl. Combine with all the remaining ingredients and mix well with your hands. This mixture will be a little thick, but that's perfectly fine.

- Place the mixture in a greased, nonstick 10-inch x 5-inch/ 25-cm x 13-cm loaf pan and bake in the oven for approximately 45 minutes, or until the internal temperature reaches 160°F/71°C and the top is golden brown. Remove from the oven and let cool for a few minutes.

- When cool enough to handle, carefully unmold the loaf. Slice, serve with Tabouleh (see page 114), and enjoy while imagining you're gazing into the Mediterranean Sea!

For the Meatloaf

½ cup fine bulgur wheat
1 cup cold water
2 (16-oz./450 g) cans garbanzo beans (chickpeas), rinsed and drained
¾ cup panko bread crumbs
¾ cup finely diced yellow onion
½ cup chopped curly parsley
⅓ cup crushed garlic
3½ tbsp. strained fresh lemon juice
3 tbsp. extra virgin olive oil
2 large eggs, lightly beaten
1¼ tsp. ground cumin
1¼ tsp. ground coriander
1¼ tsp. paprika
1 tsp. coarse sea salt
canola or vegetable oil spray, for greasing
Tabouleh (see page 114), for serving

OMEGA-3 LOAF

Servings: 6

After creating several red meat- and poultry-based meatloaves, it seemed only right to make one with salmon. We use wild-caught Alaskan salmon in The Meatloaf Bakery, but any kind of fresh or frozen salmon will work. We add a touch of wasabi to Garlic Spuds for the perfect accompaniment. If you like subtle Asian influences with classic seafood garnishes, such as lemon and dill, then you'll adore Omega-3 Loaf—all the while getting a healthy dose of those essential fatty acids!

TO MAKE

- First roast the garlic for the Garlic Wasabi Potatoes, following the recipe on page 126. Reduce the oven to 375°F/190°C.

- Skin the salmon fillets and cut into ½-inch/1-cm chunks. Pulse for a few minutes in a food processor to break the chunks down further. In a large bowl, combine the salmon with all the remaining loaf ingredients and mix well until all the ingredients are evenly distributed.

- Divide the salmon mixture into 6 portions and place in a lightly greased, large nonstick 6-cup cupcake/muffin pan. Round the top of each cupcake with your hands to form a dome. Bake in the oven for approximately 30 to 35 minutes, or until the internal temperature reaches 160°F/71°C and the cupcake tops are golden brown. Remove from the oven and let cool for a few minutes.

- While the cupcakes are baking and cooling slightly, finish preparing the Garlic Wasabi Potatoes, following the recipe on page 126.

- When cool enough to handle, unmold the cupcakes carefully and set on a flat surface in preparation for "frosting." Insert an open star pastry tip into a 12 to 14-inch/30 to 35-cm pastry bag and fill with the hot Garlic Wasabi Spuds (use caution, because the bag can be hot to the touch). Create a spiral design just like your favorite soft-serve ice cream and finish with lemon zest and dill sprigs. Serve with Lemon–Dill Sauce (see page 156).

A close relation to horseradish, wasabi packs an even stronger punch, so add to your potatoes with caution until it tastes just right. Unlike that in chili, though, the "heat" in wasabi is water- rather than oil-based, so if you've overdone it, just a mouthful of water will cool you down.

For the Meatloaf

1 batch Garlic Wasabi Potatoes
(see page 126), for topping
1¼ lb./550 g fresh or frozen salmon
fillets, thawed if frozen
⅔ cup finely diced yellow onion
½ cup finely diced celery
1 tbsp. minced garlic
½ cup chopped curly parsley
2 tbsp. chopped fresh dill, plus extra
sprigs for garnishing
2 cups butter cracker crumbs
4 tbsp. unsalted butter, softened
and diced
½ cup strained fresh lemon juice
¼ cup 2% milk
2 large eggs, lightly beaten
2 tbsp. mayonnaise
1 tsp. low-sodium soy sauce
½ tsp. paprika
1 tsp. coarse sea salt
1 tsp. black pepper
canola or vegetable oil spray,
for greasing
lemon zest, for garnishing
Lemon–Dill Sauce (see page 156),
for serving

TO CATCH A TUNA LOAF

Servings: 6

One of my favorite pastimes is creating meatloaf recipes from foods I've eaten in restaurants, friends' homes, or family gatherings. This particular recipe was inspired by a delicious tuna sandwich at a favorite spot in Chicago. I liked it so much that I immediately began crafting a recipe. It came together easily because in my mind, you can never go wrong with kalamata olives, fresh lemon juice, parsley, and onion. What a catch!

TO MAKE

- First roast and then mash the garlic for the Garlic Spuds, following the recipe on page 126. Reduce the oven to 375°F/190°C.

- Place the tuna in a large bowl and break it up with a fork. Add all the remaining loaf ingredients and mix well.

- Divide the loaf mixture into 6 portions and place in a lightly greased, large nonstick 6-cup cupcake/muffin pan. Round the top of each cupcake with your hands to form a dome. Bake in the oven for approximately 30 to 35 minutes, or until the internal temperature reaches 160°F/71°C and the cupcake tops are golden brown. Remove from the oven and let cool for a few minutes.

- While the cupcakes are baking and cooling slightly, finish preparing the Garlic Spuds, following the recipe on page 126.

- When cool enough to handle, unmold the cupcakes carefully and set on a flat surface in preparation for "frosting." Scoop the hot Garlic Spuds onto the tops of the cupcakes. Using a teaspoon, make a shallow indentation in each potato topping. Fill the indentations with diced red bell pepper, olives, and scallions.

For the Meatloaf
2 (12-oz./350 g) cans white or light tuna packed in water, drained
¾ cup finely diced red onion
¾ cup finely diced celery
¼ cup finely diced red bell pepper, plus extra for topping
¼ cup rinsed and drained capers
¼ cup chopped kalamata olives, plus extra for topping
1½ cups panko bread crumbs
½ cup chopped curly parsley
½ cup strained fresh lemon juice
6 tbsp. extra virgin olive oil
2 large eggs, lightly beaten
½ tsp. black pepper
¼ tsp. fine sea salt
canola or vegetable oil spray, for greasing

For the Topping
1 batch Garlic Spuds (see page 126)
diced scallions

SEASONAL SPECIALTIES

Drawing inspiration from seasonally available ingredients and holidays, here is a selection of recipes for your favorite times of the year, from fall favorite Chili Chili Bang Bang to springtime Lamb-A-Licious Loaf.

CHILI CHILI BANG BANG

Servings: 10 to 12

Lots of wonderful ingredients go into this very special creation. Chili Chili Bang Bang is loaded with beef, beans, cheese, and spices. Not too spicy yet with a nice little kick, it's topped with a layer of Cheesy Cornbread. Enjoy it with a crowd of friends, your family, or just by yourself. If it's a party of one, count on leftovers.

For the Meatloaf

scant 1 cup rinsed and drained canned kidney beans
scant 1 cup rinsed and drained canned black beans
1½ lb./680 g ground chuck beef
2 cups diced tomatoes well drained through cheesecloth
⅔ cup finely diced yellow onion
½ cup finely diced celery
1 tbsp. finely chopped garlic
¾ cup crushed oyster crackers
¾ cup dry white bread crumbs
½ cup panko bread crumbs
⅔ cup shredded yellow cheddar cheese
⅔ cup shredded white cheddar cheese
½ cup tomato paste
½ cup ketchup
2 large eggs, lightly beaten
2 tbsp. sour cream
1¼ tbsp. seeded and chopped jalapeño pepper
1¼ tbsp. chili powder
⅛ tsp. cayenne pepper
½ tbsp. packed light brown sugar
1 tsp. coarse sea salt
⅛ tsp. black pepper
canola or vegetable oil spray, for greasing
1 batch unbaked Cheesy Cornbread batter (see page 146), for topping
Scallion Sour Cream (see page 157), for serving

TO MAKE

- Preheat the oven to 375°F/190°C.

- Lightly pulse first the kidney beans and then the black beans in a food processor until coarsely mashed. Place the beans in a large bowl, combine with all the remaining meatloaf ingredients (except the topping), and mix well with your hands.

- Fill a greased, nonstick 13-inch x 9-inch x 2-inch/33-cm x 23-cm x 5-cm baking pan with the meatloaf mixture and smooth the top with your hands or a cake spatula. Bake in the oven for approximately 15 minutes.

- While the meatloaf is baking, prepare the Cheesy Cornbread batter, following the recipe on page 146.

- Remove the partly cooked meatloaf from the oven and spread a layer about ½ to ¾-inch/1 to 2-cm thick of the Cheesy Cornbread batter over the top. Return to the oven and bake for an additional 20 to 25 minutes. Near the end of the baking time, sprinkle the reserved yellow cheddar cheese (as specified in the Cheesy Cornbread recipe) over the top of the meatloaf and bake for a final 5 minutes—the cornbread should be a light golden brown and firm to the touch, and the meatloaf mixture should have an internal temperature of 160°F/71°C. Let cool for a few minutes, then slice and serve with fresh Scallion Sour Cream (see page 157).

LOAFER KABOBS

Servings: about 24 skewers

These are a perfect hot weather, grill-ready treat. During a huge outdoor event, we fed thousands of festivalgoers these delicious kabobs. Fire up your grill, grab a beer, and start skewering! I've provided two ways to prepare Loafer Kabobs, so pick which method works best for you. Try the Chicken Shish Kaloaf for a great nonred-meat option.

TO MAKE

- First prepare the marinated veggies. Cut all the vegetables into 1 to 1½-inch/2.5 to 4-cm chunks for skewering. Toss lightly with extra virgin olive oil, then season with garlic, the dried herbs, and salt and pepper. (Firmer vegetables, such as the carrots, can be precooked in a microwave or steamed to soften before grilling; corn on the cob, if that's one of your choices, would definitely need precooking.) Set aside while you prepare the meatloaf mixture.

COOKING OPTION 1 (meatloaf mixture baked ahead of time):

- Preheat the oven to 350°F/180°C.

- Mix the bread crumbs with the milk in a bowl to soften. In a separate bowl, beat the eggs lightly, then add the ketchup, Worcestershire and barbecue sauces, garlic, chives, Italian seasoning, paprika, salt, and pepper. In a large bowl, combine the ground meats, onion, celery, red bell pepper, and parsley, and then mix well with your hands. Add the breadcrumb-and-egg mixture and mix lightly with your hands.

- Roll the meatloaf mixture into balls about 1½ inches/4 cm in diameter. Place on a lightly greased nonstick sheet pan or cookie sheet and bake for approximately 25 to 30 minutes, or until the internal temperature reaches 160°F/71°C and the meatballs are browned, turning them a couple of times during the baking time. Remove from the oven and cool completely. Thread them onto 8 to 10-inch/20 to 25-cm metal skewers, alternating with the marinated veggies. (The ready-to-go kabobs may be kept in refrigerator for grilling later.)

- Prepare a gas or charcoal grill to cook with indirect heat—the grill temperature should be 350 to 375°F/180 to 190°C. Place the skewers directly on the grill to reheat, close the cover, and cook for 15 to 20 minutes, or until the internal temperature reaches 165°F/74°C. Turn the skewers frequently to prevent burning.

COOKING OPTION 2 (cooked entirely on the grill):

- Make the meatloaf mixture and roll into balls as directed above. Prepare a gas or charcoal grill to cook with indirect heat—the grill temperature should be 350 to 375°F/180 to 190°C. Place the skewers directly on the grill, close the cover, and cook for 20 to 30 minutes, or until the internal temperature reaches 160°F/71°C. Turn the skewers frequently to prevent burning.

For the Meatloaf

2 cups dry white bread crumbs
⅔ cup 2% milk
2 large eggs
⅓ cup ketchup
2 tbsp. Worcestershire sauce
2 tsp. barbecue sauce
2 tsp. finely chopped garlic
2 tsp. finely chopped fresh chives
1 tsp. Italian seasoning
1 tsp. paprika
1 tsp. coarse sea salt
1 tsp. black pepper
1 lb./450 g ground chuck beef
1 lb./450 g ground pork
½ cup finely diced yellow onion
⅓ cup finely diced celery
¼ cup finely diced red bell pepper
⅔ cup finely chopped curly or
   Italian parsley
canola or vegetable oil spray,
   for greasing

For the Marinated Veggies

any favorite fresh vegetables, such as:
2 zucchini
2 yellow or other summer squash
1 red bell pepper
1 yellow bell pepper
1 green bell pepper
1 red or sweet onion
12 or so cherry tomatoes
2 carrots
marinade ingredients, to taste:
extra virgin olive oil
minced garlic
dried oregano
dried basil
coarse sea salt and black pepper

LAMB-A-LICIOUS LOAF

Servings: 6 to 8

This meatloaf brings together so many wonderful Mediterranean-inspired ingredients. It's fragrant, exotic, and oh so flavorful. I particularly love the sweet onions, kalamata olives, and feta cheese highlights. Enjoy this at the holidays or any special time. It makes a beautiful presentation in a phyllo pastry log served with Tzatziki and an extra helping of tomato sauce.

TO MAKE

- Preheat the oven to 350°F/180°C.

- In a small bowl, combine the pine nuts, rosemary, oregano, mint, thyme, salt, and pepper. In a separate bowl, stir together the feta, spinach, onion, olives, and garlic until well blended. In a large bowl, gently mix the ground lamb and tomato sauce, then add the bread crumbs, egg, and extra virgin olive oil with the pine nut mixture and feta-spinach mixture. Mix well with your hands and set aside.

- Now you're ready to begin working with the phyllo pastry dough. It's best to finish making the meatloaf mixture before rolling out the phyllo so that it doesn't dry out.

- Cover a sheet pan or cookie sheet with parchment paper and lightly spray with canola or vegetable oil. Layer the sheets of phyllo pastry dough on the prepared pan, brushing each layer with melted butter, starting with the edges and working into the center. (You can also spread a thin layer of tomato sauce onto the last layer of pastry dough before adding the Lamb-A-Licious mixture if you prefer a more pronounced tomato flavor.) Spread the meatloaf filling on top of the final layer, leaving a 1-inch/2.5-cm border on each side. Roll up the pastry dough around the filling to form a log, then seal the seam by pinching lightly. Fold in the two ends to secure the meatloaf filling. Trim the excess pastry dough, if necessary. Brush the entire log with more melted butter and turn seam-side down.

- Bake in the oven for 35 minutes, gently covering the log with aluminum foil toward the end of the baking time if it's starting to brown too quickly. Uncover, if necessary, and bake for an additional 10 to 15 minutes until the internal temperature reaches 160°F/71°C and the phyllo is golden brown. Serve with Tzatziki (see page 158), and extra tomato sauce, if you like.

For the Meatloaf
¼ cup finely chopped pine nuts
1 tsp. crushed dried rosemary
1 tsp. dried oregano
1½ tsp. chopped fresh mint
1 tsp. chopped fresh thyme leaves
1 tsp. coarse sea salt
1 tsp. black pepper
¾ cup crumbled feta cheese
1 cup thawed, well drained, and
    chopped frozen spinach
½ cup finely diced sweet onion
⅓ cup drained and finely chopped
    kalamata olives
1 tbsp. minced garlic
1½ lb./680g ground lamb
¾ cup tomato sauce, plus extra for
    spreading and serving (optional)
1 cup dry white bread crumbs
1 large egg, lightly beaten
2 tsp. extra virgin olive oil
canola or vegetable oil spray,
    for greasing
Tzatziki (see page 158), for serving

For the Phyllo Pastry Wrapping
5 sheets frozen phyllo pastry dough,
    thawed
about 6 tbsp. unsalted butter, melted

CHICKEN MU SHU LOAF

Servings: 6 to 8

Like several of my other recipes, this one is inspired by something I often eat—Mu Shu Chicken. It combines traditional Asian spices, water chestnuts, garlic, and a little sesame oil. The swirl of rice vermicelli and fresh plum sauce between the layers and on top of the cake is the perfect finishing touch. And what a tasty and colorful dipping sauce those plums make!

TO MAKE

- Preheat the oven to 375°F/190°C.

- In a bowl, combine the cabbage, scallions, carrot, water chestnuts, garlic, ginger, red pepper flakes, salt, and pepper. Add the sesame oil and hoisin and soy sauces and stir to coat the vegetables.

- In a large bowl, combine the chicken, bread crumbs, and eggs. Add the vegetable mixture and mix well with your hands.

- Grease two nonstick 8-inch/20-cm round cake pans. Fill each pan with approximately one-half of the meatloaf mixture. Smooth the tops with your hands or a cake spatula. Bake in the oven for approximately 20 to 30 minutes, or until the internal temperature reaches 165°F/74°C and the meatloaf tops are golden brown. Remove from the oven and let cool for a few minutes.

- While the meatloaf layers are baking and cooling slightly, make the plum sauce. In a saucepan, combine the plums, red onion, lemon juice, sugar, and water and simmer for about 20 to 25 minutes until the plums and onion are tender. Bring to a boil and continue boiling for about 5 minutes until the sauce has thickened. Remove from the heat and blend with an immersion blender until smooth. Add the hoisin sauce, gradually tasting while doing so, then season with salt and pepper. The sauce should be a bright rosy pink, particularly if the plums are ruby red.

- Prepare the rice vermicelli, according to the package instructions. (This can typically be found in the Asian section of your supermarket or in an Asian market.) Drain thoroughly, then toss with as much or as little plum sauce as you like.

For the Meatloaf
1¼ cups chopped cabbage
¾ cup finely chopped scallions (white and green parts), plus extra for garnishing
½ cup finely diced carrot
3 tbsp. drained and finely diced canned water chestnuts
1 tbsp. minced garlic
1 tbsp. finely diced fresh ginger
¼ tsp. red pepper flakes
½ tsp. coarse sea salt
¼ tsp. black pepper
1½ tsp. sesame oil
¼ cup hoisin sauce
1 tbsp. low-sodium soy sauce
2 lb./900 g ground chicken
1 cup panko bread crumbs
2 large eggs, lightly beaten
canola or vegetable oil spray, for greasing
1 lb./450 g dry rice vermicelli noodles
sesame seeds, for garnishing

For the Plum Sauce
6 medium red plums, skins on, cut into ½-inch/1-cm pieces
1 cup finely diced red onion
¼ cup plus 1 tbsp. strained fresh lemon juice, or to taste
¾ cup granulated sugar
¾ cup water
1½ tbsp. hoisin sauce, or to taste
coarse sea salt and black pepper, to taste

- When cool enough to handle, carefully unmold the meatloaf layers. Place one Chicken Mu Shu Loaf layer on a nonstick sheet pan or cookie sheet. Cover it with a layer of the vermicelli/plum sauce mixture. Top with the second meatloaf layer and finish with a final layer of vermicelli/plum sauce. You may also add extra plum sauce in between the layers, depending upon how much sauce you prefer. Let cool completely, then cover and refrigerate until ready to serve. Reheat according to the instructions on page 14. Garnish the hot meatloaf with scallions and sesame seeds, and serve with the remaining plum sauce on the side.

- If you prefer, you can skip the noodles, bake the meatloaf mixture in a greased, nonstick 10-inch x 5-inch/25-cm x 13-cm loaf pan for 20 to 30 minutes, then brush the top with some of the plum sauce to glaze and bake for an additional 10 to 15 minutes, or until the internal temperature reaches 165°F/74°C. Simply serve with jasmine rice, laced with scallions and sesame seeds, on the side along with the remaining plum sauce.

BBQ PICNIC LOAF

Servings: 6

What's better than barbecued chicken, baked beans, and potato salad during those warm-weather months? Now you can enjoy your favorite summer foods all year round. Sweet, smoky, and tangy, this recipe is packed with flavor. Top the loaf with Red Potato Mashers and a mound of fried onions, and you'll be the hit of the picnic.

For the Meatloaf

⅓ cup apple cider vinegar
¼ cup tomato paste
1 tbsp. ketchup
1 tbsp. Dijon mustard
1 tbsp. Worcestershire sauce
1 tbsp. liquid smoke
¼ cup packed light brown sugar
1 tbsp. smoked paprika
1 tsp. onion powder
1 tsp. coarse kosher salt
½ tsp. black pepper
1 lb./450 g ground chicken
15-oz./425 g can white beans, rinsed and drained
2 cups panko bread crumbs
1 large egg, lightly beaten
¾ cup finely diced onion
½ cup finely diced celery
½ cup finely diced green bell pepper
1 tbsp. minced garlic
¾ cup shredded sharp yellow cheddar cheese
canola or vegetable oil spray, for greasing
barbecue sauce, for serving

For the Topping

1 batch Red Potato Mashers (see page 132), plus an extra 1 batch for serving (optional)
1 batch Fried Shoestring Onions (see page 138)

TO MAKE

- Preheat the oven to 375°F/190°C.

- In a bowl, whisk together the vinegar, tomato paste, ketchup, mustard, Worcestershire sauce, and liquid smoke with a fork or wire whisk. Gradually add the brown sugar, paprika, onion powder, salt, and pepper and continue whisking until well mixed. Combine all the other meatloaf ingredients in a large bowl. Stir in the sauce mixture and mix well with your hands.

- Place the meatloaf mixture in a greased, nonstick 10-inch x 5-inch/25-cm x 13-cm loaf pan and smooth the top with your hands or a cake spatula. Bake in the oven for approximately 45 to 50 minutes, or until the internal temperature reaches 165°F/74°C and the top is golden brown. Remove from the oven and let cool for a few minutes.

- While the meatloaf is baking and cooling slightly, prepare the Red Potato Mashers, following the recipe on page 132, and then the Fried Shoestring Onions, following the recipe on page 138.

- When cool enough to handle, carefully unmold the meatloaf. Using a cake spatula, spread a layer of the hot Red Potato Mashers over the loaf. Top with the Fried Shoestring Onions, then slice and serve with an extra scoop of the potatoes (make a double batch of the Red Potato Mashers to be sure you have plenty) and your favorite barbecue sauce on the side.

Liquid smoke is key to adding that special barbecue taste. If you ever wondered just what was in it—it really IS smoke, produced by condensing the smoke given off by burning wood and passing it through water to rid it of impurities.

CHICKEN SHISH KALOAF

Servings: 6

I love, love, love this recipe! It's fresh and light, loaded with lemon, and dairy-free if you don't add the Garlic Spuds. I incorporated all of the spices and herbs I ate while growing up, and Chicken Shish Kaloaf was born. It's a bakery favorite and a perfect alternative to other more robust recipes. Try it with Garlic Spuds and serve with Shish Kamint Sauce.

TO MAKE

- Make the Shish Kamint Sauce in advance by whisking together all the ingredients in a bowl with a fork or wire whisk. Cover with plastic wrap and store in the refrigerator until ready to serve.

- Roast and then mash the garlic for the Garlic Spuds, following the recipe on page 126. Reduce the oven to 375°F/190°C.

- In a bowl, combine the onion, garlic, parsley, thyme, paprika, and salt. Set aside. In a large bowl, combine the chicken, lemon juice, extra virgin olive oil, bread crumbs, and eggs. Add the vegetable mixture and mix well with your hands. Just wait until you smell that garlic and lemon.

- Divide the meatloaf mixture into 6 portions and place in a lightly greased, large nonstick 6-cup cupcake/muffin pan. Round the top of each meatloaf cupcake with your hands to form a dome. Bake in the oven for 30 to 40 minutes, or until the internal temperature reaches 165°F/74°C and the cupcake tops are golden brown. Remove from the oven and cool for a few minutes.

- While the meatloaf cupcakes are baking and cooling slightly, finish preparing the Garlic Spuds, according to the recipe on page 126.

- When cool enough to handle, unmold the meatloaf cupcakes carefully and set on paper towels to remove any excess moisture. Insert any pastry tip into a 12 to 14-inch/30 to 35-cm pastry bag and fill with the hot Garlic Spuds (use caution, because the bag can be hot to the touch). Try your hand at swirls, petals, or whatever design you like. And if time doesn't permit, just top each Chicken Shish Kaloaf cupcake with a small scoop of Garlic Spuds (or use Yukon Smashers, see page 124, instead for a variation). Sprinkle a little sumac onto each cupcake for that finishing touch. Serve with the chilled Shish Kamint Sauce.

For the Meatloaf
1 batch Garlic Spuds (see page 126), for topping
1¼ cups finely diced red onion
3 tbsp. minced garlic
¾ cup finely chopped curly parsley
1 tsp. finely chopped fresh thyme leaves
½ tsp. paprika
2 tsp. coarse sea salt
2 lb./900 g ground chicken
⅓ cup strained fresh lemon juice
¼ cup extra virgin olive oil
1⅓ cups panko bread crumbs
2 large eggs, lightly beaten
canola or vegetable oil spray, for greasing
dried sumac, for sprinkling

For the Shish Kamint Sauce
2 cups unsweetened plain yogurt
2 tbsp. chopped fresh mint
1½ tbsp. crushed garlic
fine sea salt and white pepper, to taste

Not everyone loves a strong mint flavor, so I've suggested using a small quantity of mint in the sauce to keep the taste subtle. I also prefer spearmint because it's not as pungent as peppermint. If you prefer your sauce a bit stronger, simply add more mint or choose peppermint.

LITE BITES

From starters such as Soup-A-Roma and Cynthia's Salad to The Meatloaf Bakery's trademark Loafies, these will serve you well as a main dish or a tempting appetizer.

SOUP-A-ROMA

Servings: 4 to 6

Tomato soup is wonderful on its own, but load it with Loaf-A-Roma Bites and pasta and you really have something special. The whipping cream creates a velvety texture, while the basil adds just the right touch. Pour your favorite Italian red wine, and enjoy three of the best comfort foods—tomato soup, meatloaf, and pasta—all in one delicious bowl. I love it with crusty olive bread and my Fennel and Blood Orange Salad.

TO MAKE

- Preheat the oven to 375°F/190°C.

- Prepare half of the Loaf-A-Roma meatloaf mixture, following the recipe on page 60. Form the mixture into individual meatballs about 1 inch/2.5 cm in diameter—this should yield about 30 meatballs. Place the meatballs in a lightly greased, shallow baking pan and bake in the oven for 20 to 25 minutes, or until the internal temperature reaches 160°F/71°C.

- While the meatballs are baking, cook the pasta according to the package instructions until al dente. Drain well and set aside.

- In a large saucepan, add the crushed tomatoes, tomato sauce, basil, garlic, sugar, salt, and pepper. Simmer on low heat until hot and well mixed. Slowly add the whipping cream and continue stirring— be sure to stir constantly to prevent burning at the bottom of the pan. Remove from the heat and blend with an immersion blender. (If you like your soup thick and chunky, you can eliminate this step.)

- Return to low heat and add a little water (½ cup or less), if necessary, to thin down the soup. Add the cooked Loaf-A-Roma Bites and heat thoroughly. Immediately before serving, add the cooked pasta. Ladle into soup bowls and garnish with fresh basil and a sprinkling of Parmesan.

Note: If you'd like to make a full batch of Loaf-A-Roma, portion the remaining mixture into a lightly greased, 6-cup nonstick cupcake/muffin pan. Round the top of each cupcake with your hands to form a dome; bake in the oven for approximately 20 to 30 minutes or until internal temperature reaches 160°F/71°C.

For the Soup

½ batch uncooked Loaf-A-Roma meatloaf mixture (see page 60)

canola or vegetable oil spray, for greasing

about 1 cup dry small pasta shapes, such as shells, fusilli, farfalle, gemelli, or rotini (to yield 2 cups cooked)

2 (15-oz./425-g) cans crushed tomatoes

¾ cup tomato sauce

¾ cup fresh basil cut into long thin strips, plus extra for garnishing

1 tsp. crushed garlic

½ tsp. granulated sugar

½ tsp. coarse kosher salt

¼ tsp. freshly ground black pepper

½ cup whipping cream

grated Parmesan cheese, for garnishing

FENNEL AND BLOOD ORANGE SALAD

Servings: 4 to 6

Fennel, with its subtle licorice essence, may not be for everyone, but pair it with cured black olives, blood oranges, a fruity olive oil, and fresh lemon juice and you'll have a new appreciation for this oft-forgotten vegetable. I love it, and recommend it with Loaf-A-Roma and Soup-A-Roma.

For the Salad

2 fennel bulbs, outer layer discarded and sliced into very thin strips
2 large blood oranges (or use navel or Minneola oranges)
½ cup pitted and halved oil-cured ripe black olives
¼ cup extra virgin olive oil
2–3 tbsp. strained fresh lemon juice
fine sea salt and freshly ground black pepper, to taste

TO MAKE

• Place the prepared fennel slices in icy cold water until ready to mix with the rest of the ingredients.

• Peel the oranges. Using a paring knife, trim off the white pith and remove each orange segment from the membrane on either side of it. If this technique proves to be a challenge, simply slice the orange into ¼-inch/5-mm thick circles and then quarter. Be sure to remove any seeds.

• Drain the fennel and add to a bowl with the olives and oranges, and lightly toss together. Drizzle the extra virgin olive oil and lemon juice over the salad. Toss lightly again and season with salt and pepper.

In olden times, fennel water was fed to infants to help them digest their food properly; today, like mint, fennel is recognized as being good both for the digestion and as a breath freshener. This light, crunchy salad brings out its very particular and special flavor.

CYNTHIA'S SALAD

Servings: 4 to 6

It may not be the most original name, but "Cynthia's Salad" is what everyone calls my tossed salad with red wine-lemon vinaigrette. I wish I could say it was my recipe, but I took my inspiration from my mother, who made it just about every night while I was growing up. The first step in this ritual was smashing the garlic clove in the bottom of the bowl with a little salt. That and peeling the carrots was my job. My mother was faster at everything than I, so she usually finished it up and added the oil, lemon, wine vinegar, and seasonings in just the right amounts. Of course, I was the official taster.

TO MAKE

- First is the garlic preparation. This technique may not be professional culinary practice, but it sure does work. Place a little salt in the bottom of your salad bowl. Add the garlic clove and, using the end of a wooden knife handle or a pestle, smash the garlic until it's a fine paste (the salt helps to break up the garlic).

- Add the prepared vegetables to the salad bowl, saving the lettuce and tomatoes for last. Sprinkle with the mint and parsley. Drizzle the extra virgin olive oil, lemon juice, and wine vinegar over the salad (but if you choose to include the Dijon mustard, first whisk it with the olive oil, lemon juice, and wine vinegar). Mix well and taste, then add more lemon juice or wine vinegar, if you like. Season with salt and pepper.

For the Salad
½–1 garlic clove, peeled
4–5 radishes, thinly sliced
3–4 scallions, sliced
1–2 carrots, sliced
½ large red or yellow bell pepper, seeded and diced
½ medium cucumber, sliced
1 head Romaine lettuce, torn into salad-size pieces
2–3 Roma tomatoes, cut into 1-inch/2.5-cm pieces
1 tbsp. chopped fresh mint
1 tbsp. chopped fresh curly parsley
¼ cup extra virgin olive oil (or use canola or vegetable oil, if you prefer)
2–3 tbsp. fresh lemon juice, or to taste
2 tbsp. red wine vinegar, or to taste
½ tsp. Dijon mustard (optional)
fine sea salt and freshly ground black pepper, to taste

TABOULEH

Servings: 6 to 8

We all have memories of our favorite dishes. I can remember picking the stems off bunches and bunches of parsley, soaking and rinsing the parsley multiple times to remove any dirt, waiting for it to dry, and then watching my mother chop it by hand—those were the days before food processors. A frequent mealtime and party ritual in our house, Tabouleh prep is forever ingrained in my memory. I hope you enjoy it as much as I do!

TO MAKE

- In a bowl, soak the bulgur wheat in the water for about 10 to 15 minutes until softened. In the meantime, prepare the parsley by picking the leaves off the stems. Wash well in cold water to remove any dirt and then spin out the water using a salad spinner (see page 12). Lay the parsley on paper towels and pat lightly with the towels to dry thoroughly. Chop in a food processor (or by hand, if you prefer) and place in a salad bowl.

- Squeeze out any excess water from the bulgur wheat and add to the parsley. Add the scallions and mint. Gradually add the oil (feel free to choose whichever oil you prefer; both work well) and lemon juice. Depending upon your tastes, you can adjust the oil and lemon up or down. (I prefer tabouleh to be on the drier side with a lot of lemon.) Season with salt and pepper.

- Scoop the tabouleh onto a platter and spread the tomatoes over the top. Serve with romaine lettuce leaves—they make perfect scoops.

For the Tabouleh
½ cup fine bulgur wheat
1 cup cold water
about 2 large bunches fresh curly
    parsley (to yield 6 cups chopped)
½ cup chopped scallions (white and
    green parts)
½ cup chopped fresh mint
½ cup canola oil or extra virgin olive oil
¼ cup strained fresh lemon juice,
    or to taste
fine sea salt and freshly ground black
    pepper, to taste
1½ cups diced tomatoes
romaine lettuce leaves, for serving

LOAFER POPS

Pop, pop goes the loaf. These lollipop-size meatloaf treats are great for kids and the young at heart. Complete with potato frosting and a handy stick handle for easy eating, Loafer Pops are delicious additions to any party setting. Choose your favorite recipes and start popping!

TO MAKE

- Preheat the oven to 375°F/190°C.

- Roll just about any of the meatloaf mixtures into individual balls about 2 inches/5 cm in diameter. Place on a lightly greased, nonstick cookie sheet and bake for approximately 20 to 25 minutes, or until the internal temperature reaches 160°F/71°C for meat, seafood, or vegetarian mixtures, or 165°F/74°C for poultry, turning them a couple of times during the baking time. Remove from the oven and let cool for a few minutes.

- When cool enough to handle, transfer the balls to paper towels to absorb any moisture. If you plan to serve immediately, insert any star or wide pastry tip into a 12 to 14-inch/30 to 35-cm pastry bag, fill with your chosen hot potato recipe (see pages 124–33; use caution, because the bag can be hot to the touch), and pipe onto the top of the baked Loafer Pops. Insert a round 8-inch/20-cm-long wooden stick into each and serve on a flat platter with my suggested dipping sauce for the meatloaf recipe you've chosen, or one of your favorites.

- Loafer Pops can be made ahead of time, cooled, and stored in the refrigerator in a covered container, and then heated when you're ready to enjoy. Simply place them on a lightly greased, nonstick cookie sheet and heat in an oven preheated to 375°F/190°C for approximately 15 to 20 minutes until golden brown, or the internal temperature reaches 165°F/74°C.

Cute and healthy kids' party food? These darling pops are the answer. The neat presentation will appeal to the children, while parents will appreciate one treat that won't induce a sugar high. I guarantee there won't be any left over.

LOAFIES

If cupcakes, pies, cakes, and loaves just aren't enough, try your hand at Loafies! These bite-size versions of my distinctive meatloaf creations are perfect hors d'oeuvres for your next event or gathering. It's best to make these in advance and then simply heat them up when you're ready to party!

Try snacking on these delightful miniature variations of my meatloaf recipes. All of them are great choices for parties, kids' events, movie nights, or fast and fun-to-eat lunches.

BAKED LOAFIES

• Preheat the oven to 375°F/190°C.

• For most meatloaf recipes, form the mixture into balls about 1 inch/2.5 cm in diameter and place each in a premade or store-bought ready-to-bake mini savory pastry shell (check online sources to purchase, or if you'd like, try your hand at making profiteroles or mini buns for sliders). Set on a nonstick cookie sheet and bake in the oven for approximately 20 to 25 minutes, or until the internal temperatures reaches 160°F/71°C for meat, seafood, or vegetarian mixtures, or 165°F/74°C for poultry. Remove from the oven, transfer to a wire rack, and let cool completely.

• Top each Loafie with a dollop of your chosen chilled potato recipe (see pages 124–33), MACnificent Pasta (see page 78), or Herbed Stuffing (see page 51). Cover gently and store in the refrigerator until you need them. When ready to serve, put them on a lightly greased cookie sheet and heat in an oven preheated to 375°F/190°C for approximately 10 minutes until golden brown, or the internal temperature reaches 165°F/74°C.

DEEP-FRIED LOAFIES

• MACnificent Pasta (see page 78) and Yentl Lentl Loaf (see page 84) also make wonderful snacks when lightly fried. Form the cooled pasta and sauce mixture or loaf mixture into balls about 1 inch/2.5 cm in diameter and then cover and chill in the refrigerator for a few hours. Now you are ready for the three-step frying process.

• Place about 2 cups all-purpose flour, 4 lightly beaten eggs, and 2 cups panko bread crumbs in separate bowls. In a large, heavy saucepan, heat about 8 cups vegetable or canola oil to 375°F/190°C, or use an electric deep-fryer. One at a time, coat each ball with flour, then beaten egg, and finally bread crumbs. Fry in the hot oil, in batches, for about 30 seconds until golden brown.

• Remove the Loafies from the oil and place on paper towels to drain. Serve as soon as they are cool enough to handle (but remember they'll be hot on the inside).

KABOB-WICHES

Ready for a summer picnic, boating event, or just a balcony get-together with friends? How about cold meatloaf triangles? Kabob-Wiches are made with Chicken Shish Kaloaf, pita bread triangles, a grape tomato, and a bit of lettuce. Drizzle on Shish Kamint Sauce and you've got a light and delicious snack. Pick your favorite meatloaf recipes such as Holy Moly Chicken Frijole, Kickin' Cajun Loaf, or Omega-3 Loaf and create your own party snacks.

TO MAKE

- Preheat the oven to 375°F/190°C.

- Roll the meatloaf mixture into balls about 1 inch/2.5 cm in diameter. Place on a lightly greased, nonstick cookie sheet and bake for approximately 20 to 25 minutes, or until the internal temperature reaches 160°F/71°C for meat, seafood, or vegetarian mixtures, or 165°F/74°C for poultry, turning them a couple of times during the baking time. Remove from the oven and let cool for a few minutes.

- When cool enough to handle, transfer the meatloaf balls to paper towels to absorb any moisture and let cool completely. Refrigerate in a covered container until you are ready to assemble and serve.

- Cut small triangles of pita, naan, or any sturdy bread. Layer with the lettuce, meatballs, and a grape tomato, then hold together with a toothpick—those with the frilly ends work well. Alternatively, try rolling the meatballs and garnishes (pickles, bell peppers, tomatoes—whatever sounds good) in a small wrap and then fasten together with a toothpick. Pile them up on a platter and enjoy with any chilled dipping sauce.

For the Kabob-Wiches
1 batch uncooked Chicken Shish Kaloaf meatloaf mixture (see page 104)
pita, naan, or other firm bread
Romaine or leaf lettuce leaves
grape tomatoes

SOMETHING ON THE SIDE

A little something on the side is always a good idea. Fresh twists on traditional vegetable dishes, Cheesy Cornbread, and, of course, mashed potatoes, will pair with just about any meatloaf on your menu.

YUKON SMASHERS

Servings: 4 to 6

The classic mashed potato gets a little added oomph from the natural buttery quality of Yukon Gold potatoes. I prefer to leave a little skin on the spuds for visual appeal. Looking good on top of The Mother Loaf or piled in a dish, they always please.

Yukon Gold potatoes were bred from a mix of small, orange-fleshed potatoes originating in Peru and modern white varieties. Although they're a comparatively recent development, they're widely available and unbeatable for flavor.

TO MAKE

- Partly peel the potatoes, leaving some of the skin on so they look almost striped—this adds texture, color, and nutrient value. Cut the potatoes into 2-inch/5-cm cubes. Place in a large saucepan and cover with cold water. Bring to a boil on high heat, then reduce the heat and continue cooking for about 10 to 15 minutes, or until the potatoes are fork tender. In the meantime, warm the milk in a microwave.

- Drain the potatoes in a colander and return to the saucepan. Add the warm milk, softened butter, and sour cream and season to taste with salt and pepper, then mash with a potato masher—a few lumps are perfectly fine, but if you intend to try your hand at piping, it's easier if the mixture is smooth.

For the Smashers
8 Yukon Gold potatoes (about 2 lb./900 g)
2 tbsp. 2% milk
4 tbsp. unsalted butter, softened
heaping 1 tbsp. sour cream
coarse sea salt and freshly ground
    white pepper, to taste

GARLIC SPUDS

Servings: 4 to 6

Mashed potatoes are a wonderful comfort food on their own, but even the most delicious things can be improved upon. Enter Garlic Spuds. Fresh garlic, roasted and pureed, brings mashed potatoes to a more elegant level, making them black-tie appropriate for any style of cuisine.

TO MAKE

- Preheat the oven to 400°F/200°C.

- Cut off the ends of the garlic cloves and place in a shallow pan with the olive oil. Roast in the oven for approximately 15 minutes, or until the garlic is soft and golden brown. Lift the cloves out of the oil and mash well into a paste. Set aside. Feel free to dab some bread into the remaining delicious garlic-infused olive oil while you're waiting for the potatoes to boil, or preparing your meatloaf.

- Place the potatoes in a large saucepan and cover with cold water. Bring to a boil on high heat, then reduce the heat and continue cooking for about 10 to 15 minutes, or until the potatoes are fork tender. In the meantime, warm the milk in a microwave. Drain the potatoes in a colander and return to the pan. Add the warm milk, softened butter, and sour cream, and then mash with a potato masher. While the potatoes are still hot, add the reserved roasted garlic paste and continue mashing until the potatoes reach the desired consistency—smooth for shaping or piping; less smooth for scooping. Season with salt and pepper.

For the Garlic Spuds
1 oz./25 g (about 8) peeled garlic cloves
about ¼ cup olive oil
8 Russet potatoes (about 2 lb./900 g),
    peeled and cut into 2-inch/5-cm
    cubes
2 tbsp. 2% milk
4 tbsp. unsalted butter, softened
heaping 1 tbsp. sour cream
coarse sea salt and freshly ground
    white pepper, to taste

VARIATION: Garlic Wasabi Potatoes

- Make 1 batch of the Garlic Spuds, following the recipe above, mashing the potatoes until smooth and seasoning with salt and pepper. Mix ½ to 1 teaspoon wasabi powder (to taste) with 1 to 2 tablespoons milk to a paste and whip into the mashed potatoes while they are still hot. Taste the potatoes to make sure they have the right amount of heat.

CHEESY TATERS

Servings: 4 to 6

Imagine a creamy blend of three cheeses with sour cream and butter. Cheesy potatoes have never been this good. Love them alone and on No Buns About It Burger Loaf and The Father Loaf.

TO MAKE

- Place the potatoes in a large saucepan and cover with cold water. Bring to a boil on high heat, then reduce the heat and continue cooking for about 10 to 15 minutes, or until the potatoes are fork tender. In the meantime, warm the milk in a microwave.

- Drain the potatoes in a colander and return to the pan. Add the warm milk, softened butter, and sour cream, and then mash with a potato masher. While the potatoes are still hot, add the cheeses and continue mashing until they are melted. Season with salt and pepper—because these cheeses can be salty, you may not need to add any salt, perhaps only a little white pepper to bring out the flavors. As for lumps, they're totally acceptable if you don't intend to do any creative piping. However, if you'd like to try your hand with a pastry bag and your favorite decorative tip, be sure to minimize lumps, because they make piping more difficult.

VARIATION: Caraway–Horseradish Smashers

- Make 1 batch of the Cheesy Taters, following the recipe above, but replace the cheeses with 1 tbsp. plus 1 tsp. prepared (pure) horseradish and the same quantity of crushed caraway seeds—feel free to add more horseradish to taste. Continue mashing until the potatoes reach the desired consistency (smooth for piping or topping). Season with salt and pepper.

For the Cheesy Taters
8 Russet potatoes (about 2 lb./900 g), peeled and cut into 2-inch/5-cm cubes
2 tbsp. 2% milk
4 tbsp. unsalted butter, softened
1 tbsp. plus 1 tsp. sour cream
1⅓ cups shredded sharp yellow cheddar cheese
¼ cup shredded Asiago cheese
¼ cup shredded Parmesan cheese
coarse sea salt and freshly ground white pepper, to taste

WHIPPED SWEET POTATOES

Servings: 4 to 6

A few pinches of brown sugar bring out the natural sweetness in these potatoes. Whipped to fluffy perfection, they bring a beautiful balance of sweet and spicy when paired with Sassy Turkey Sausage. Or do like I do, spoon some up and simply enjoy a bowlful.

For the Whipped Sweet Potatoes
6 sweet potatoes (about 2 lb./900 g)
4 tbsp. butter, softened
1 tbsp. packed light brown sugar
2% milk, as necessary
fine sea salt and freshly ground
    black pepper, to taste

TO MAKE

- Preheat the oven to 375°F/190°C.

- Bake the sweet potatoes in the oven for 45 minutes to 1 hour until they are soft in the center (easily pierced with a fork or cake tester). Remove from the oven and let cool for a few minutes.

- When cool enough to handle, scoop the cooked potato out of the skins and into the bowl of an electric stand mixer. Add the butter and brown sugar and whip until the ingredients are well combined. Add milk as necessary to achieve the consistency you prefer while continuing to whip, and then adjust the seasoning with salt and pepper. You can mash by hand with a potato masher, if you prefer.

Sweet potatoes are high in fiber and rich in potassium and vitamin C. And they're delicious as well. Try whipping them without the butter and brown sugar for an even healthier option.

RED POTATO MASHERS

Servings: 6

Red-skinned potatoes are delicious accompaniments to any meatloaf. Add fresh chives and sour cream and you have a summertime potato perfect for my BBQ Picnic Loaf. Be sure to leave a partial peel to get some of that rosy color and texture.

TO MAKE

- Place the partly peeled potatoes in a large saucepan and cover with cold water. Bring to a boil on high heat, then reduce the heat and continue cooking for about 15 to 20 minutes, or until the potatoes are fork tender. In the meantime, warm the milk in a microwave.

- Drain the potatoes in a colander and return to the pan. Add the softened butter, sour cream, and the warm milk, gradually, adding as much as needed. Then add the chives and season with salt and pepper. Mash well with a potato masher, leaving some chunks for extra bursts of potato flavor.

For the Red Potato Mashers
12 red-skinned potatoes (about 3 lb./ 1.3 kg), partly peeled and cut into 2-inch/5-cm cubes
¼ cup or less 2% milk, as necessary
4 tbsp. unsalted butter, softened
1 tbsp. sour cream
2 tbsp. chopped fresh chives
coarse sea salt and freshly ground black pepper, to taste

ROASTED SWEET POTATOES

Servings: 6 to 8

Not only are sweet potatoes delicious, they have many health benefits. I enjoy them simply baked or prepared in this easy recipe. The herbs and olive oil add a special taste to make a great side dish.

For the Roasted Sweet Potatoes
½ cup extra virgin olive oil
2 garlic cloves, crushed
1 tbsp. dried oregano
1 tbsp. dried basil
1 tbsp. dried thyme
1 tbsp. dried marjoram
4 large sweet potatoes, peeled and cut lengthwise into wedges
coarse sea salt and freshly ground black pepper, to taste
grated Parmesan cheese, for sprinkling (optional)

TO MAKE

- Preheat the oven to 375°F/190°C.

- In a small bowl, mix together the extra virgin olive oil, garlic, and herbs. (You can add any additional herbs that you are especially fond of or, if you prefer, use premixed Italian seasoning in place of the herbs I've suggested.) Place the sweet potatoes in a large bowl, add the olive oil mixture, and toss until the potatoes are coated. Add a sprinkle of salt and pepper and mix again.

- Spread the potatoes on a cookie sheet and roast for 35 to 40 minutes, or until fork tender. Sprinkle a little Parmesan cheese on top before serving, if you like.

DIVINE POTATOES AND ONIONS

Servings: 6 to 8

Potatoes and sweet onions laced with garlicky olive oil and butter are right up there as one of my favorites, next to ice cream—and meatloaf, of course. Baked together, this combo is irresistible. Try adding a sweet potato for extra flavor. Or add a dash of paprika for color and more taste.

TO MAKE

- First prepare the garlic-infused olive oil. Preheat the oven to 400°F/200°C. Trim the ends of the garlic cloves and place in a shallow roasting pan. Add the extra virgin olive oil and toss to coat. Roast in the oven for 15 minutes, or until garlic is soft and golden brown. Strain, reserving the oil. What to do with the roasted garlic? Spread on buttered crusty French bread—delicious! Reduce the oven to 375°F/190°C.

- Layer one-third of the potatoes in the bottom of a 9-inch x 7-inch/23-cm x 18-cm baking dish. (I prefer to leave some of the skin on the potatoes to add a bit of color and texture, as well as extra nutrients.) Drizzle the reserved garlic-infused olive oil over the potatoes, followed by one-third of the butter pieces. Sprinkle some of the Herbes de Provence over the potato layer. Place a layer of onions on top of the potatoes and drizzle with more of the garlic-infused olive oil.

- Repeat layering the remaining ingredients until you have 3 layers of potatoes and 2 layers of onions (with butter and Herbes de Provence on top of the potato layers), ending with potatoes. Season with salt and pepper. Bake in the oven for 30 to 45 minutes, or until the potatoes are tender and golden on top. (I don't typically cover the dish, because I prefer the potatoes and onions golden and crispy, but you can cover it with aluminum foil for the first 20 to 25 minutes and then uncover to finish.)

For the Divine Potatoes and Onions

3–4 large Russet potatoes, partly peeled and cut into ¼-inch/5-mm thick slices
2 tbsp. salted butter, diced
1 tbsp. dried Herbes de Provence
1 large sweet onion (Vidalia or Texas), thinly sliced
fine sea salt and freshly ground black pepper, to taste

For the Garlic-Infused Olive Oil

2 oz./55 g (about 16) peeled garlic cloves
about ½ cup extra virgin olive oil

FRIED SHOESTRING ONIONS

Servings: 6

Crispy, light, and delicious—the perfect choice
for the BBQ Picnic Loaf. Can't wait to try them?
Grab a handful!

TO MAKE

- Peel the onions and cut into very thin slices, about ⅛ to ¼ inch/
  3 to 5 mm thick, then cut the slices into halves, or quarters if the
  onions are very large, to create strips.

- In a bowl, lightly beat the eggs and then beat in the milk. Combine
  the flour, salt, and pepper in a separate bowl.

- In a large, heavy saucepan, heat the vegetable or canola oil to
  375°F/190°C, or use an electric deep-fryer. Dip the onions into the
  egg-and-milk mixture until lightly coated, letting the excess drip off.
  Continue until all onions are coated. Then coat the onions, in
  batches, in the seasoned flour mixture until all have been floured.

- Fry the onions, a handful at a time, in the hot oil for approximately
  1 to 2 minutes until golden brown. Be sure to keep your eye on
  the process, because the onions will brown quickly. Carefully
  remove them from the hot oil with tongs or a slotted spoon.
  Immediately place on paper towels to drain. Finish up and serve
  immediately, seasoning with more salt and pepper, if you like.

For the Shoestring Onions
2 large onions
2 large eggs
½ cup 2% milk
2 cups all-purpose flour
1 tsp. fine sea salt, or to taste
¼ tsp. freshly ground black pepper,
  or to taste
8 cups vegetable or canola oil,
  for deep-frying

HERB-ROASTED VEGGIES

Servings: 6 to 8

Oven-roasted fresh seasonal vegetables are the best! With a little preparation beforehand (or you can purchase them precut), you'll have an easy and delicious medley of your favorites. Any fresh vegetables will work here, but I recommend the following as a starting point—just feel free to adjust the quantities, depending on how many varieties you choose.

For the Herb-Roasted Veggies

1 turnip, peeled and cut into 1-inch/2.5-cm cubes
1 carrot, cut into 1-inch/2.5-cm pieces
½ head cauliflower, cut into florets
½ head broccoli, cut into florets
6–7 Brussels sprouts, stems trimmed and outer leaves discarded
1 ear corn on the cob, cut into 3-inch/7.5-cm pieces
1 zucchini, cut into ½-inch/1-cm thick slices
1 yellow squash, cut into ½-inch/1-cm thick slices
1 red bell pepper, cut into 1-inch/2.5-cm pieces
1 yellow bell pepper, cut into 1-inch/2.5-cm pieces
1 green bell pepper, cut into 1-inch/2.5-cm pieces
1 red onion, quartered
extra virgin olive oil, for coating
coarse sea salt, to taste
crushed garlic, to taste (optional)
dried Herbes de Provence, for sprinkling

TO MAKE

• Preheat the oven to 400°F/200°C.

• In a large bowl, place the turnip, carrot, cauliflower, broccoli, Brussels sprouts, and corn. Place all the remaining, softer vegetables in a separate large bowl. Toss both batches of vegetables with enough olive oil to coat them. Season with salt, garlic (if desired), and a sprinkling of Herbes de Provence and mix well.

• Spread the firmer vegetables in a single layer in a large roasting pan and roast for 10 minutes. Remove from the oven and add the softer vegetables to the pan. Return the pan to the oven and roast for 10 minutes more, or until all the vegetables are tender.

BRUSSELS SPROUTS 'N' GRAPES

Servings: 4 to 5

It seems Brussels sprouts are either loved
or shunned. I happen to adore them, and
this recipe is simple, pretty, and very good.
The red seedless grapes add a touch of
sweetness to the slightly bitter sprouts.

For the Brussels Sprouts 'N' Grapes
2 tbsp. unsalted butter
about 30 Brussels sprouts, stems
    trimmed and outer leaves discarded,
    halved
¼ cup water
fine sea salt and freshly ground black
    pepper, to taste
1 cup red seedless grapes

TO MAKE

• Melt the butter in a large frying pan over low heat. Add the
Brussels sprouts and water and cook for about 15 to 20 minutes
until fork tender but still a bit crisp. Season with salt and pepper.
Toss with the grapes and serve immediately.

GARLIC SPINACH

Servings: 4 to 6

How about a dose of vitamins and nutrients with this tasty fresh spinach recipe? The garlic and kosher salt add so much flavor to the lightly sautéed spinach leaves. Enjoy with Lamb-A-Licious Loaf and Chicken Shish Kaloaf.

TO MAKE

• Coat a large, deep sauté pan with olive oil and heat over low heat. Add the spinach, cover, and cook for about 2 to 3 minutes until the spinach begins to wilt. Add the garlic and toss lightly. Remove from the heat and sprinkle with salt. If you like lemon, squeeze a little fresh lemon juice over the top and serve immediately.

For the Garlic Spinach
about 3 tbsp. olive oil, for coating
2–3 bunches fresh spinach, washed, drained well, and stems discarded
4–5 garlic cloves, thinly sliced
kosher salt, to taste
fresh lemon juice, to taste (optional)

MINTY CARROTS

Servings: 4 to 6

Fresh mint, lemon zest, and butter bring new appeal to the tried and true carrot. Cut them on a diagonal, and add salt and pepper, for a healthy dose of vitamin A and plenty of complementary flavors. Perfect with Lamb-A-Licious Loaf, Chicken Shish Kaloaf, or Kickin' Cajun Loaf.

TO MAKE

- Place the water in a steamer and steam the carrots for approximately 10 to 15 minutes until fork tender. Drain thoroughly and place in a bowl. Add the butter, mint, lemon juice and zest, and sugar, and then toss lightly with the carrots. Transfer to a serving platter. Finish by seasoning with salt and pepper and enjoy.

For Minty Carrots
½ cup water
1 lb./450 g carrots, cut diagonally into
  ⅛-inch/3-mm thick slices
4 tbsp. unsalted butter, diced
¼ cup chopped fresh mint
1 tbsp. strained fresh lemon juice
1 tsp. finely grated lemon zest
½ tsp. granulated sugar
coarse sea salt and freshly ground
  black pepper, to taste

RED CABBAGE SLAW

Servings: 4 to 6

This is just the prettiest little salad, tangy and refreshing as well as colorful. Enjoy it with The Sister Loaf; it also pairs nicely with a hot or cold slice of The Mother Loaf on a ciabatta roll.

For the Red Cabbage Slaw
1 small head red cabbage, thinly sliced
5–6 scallions (white and green parts), sliced diagonally
2–3 carrots, sliced diagonally
¼ cup extra virgin olive oil
juice of ½ lemon
coarse sea salt and freshly ground black pepper, to taste

TO MAKE

• Mix together the cabbage, scallions, and carrots in a large salad bowl. Add the extra virgin olive oil and lemon juice and toss to coat. Season with salt and pepper.

CHEESY CORNBREAD

Servings: 10 to 12

If you like homemade cornbread, you'll definitely love this recipe. Enhanced with cheddar cheese, it's delicious by itself as well as baked on Chili Chili Bang Bang. Dress it up with a sprinkle of your favorite shredded cheese.

TO MAKE

- Preheat your oven to 375°F/190°C.

- Melt the butter in a medium saucepan over low heat—keep your eye on this so you don't burn the butter. Remove from heat and whisk in the sugar with a wire whisk until dissolved. Then add the eggs and whisk again. In a small bowl, mix together the baking powder and milk and then add this to the butter-and-egg mixture.

- In a separate bowl, combine the cornmeal, flour, the white cheddar cheese, one-half the yellow cheddar cheese, and salt and then whisk into the butter-and-egg mixture with the wire whisk. Be sure to whisk thoroughly until all the lumps are gone and the batter is smooth.

- Pour into a lightly greased 13-inch x 9-inch x 2-inch/33-cm x 23-cm x 2-cm baking pan and bake in the oven for 15 to 20 minutes. Remove from the oven and sprinkle the reserved cheddar cheese on top. Return to the oven and bake for an additional 10 minutes, or until the top is golden brown and it passes the clean toothpick test.

Note: This recipe makes enough to top Chili Chili Bang Bang and fill a 9-inch/ 23-cm pie pan.

For the Cheesy Cornbread
2 sticks (½ lb./225 g) unsalted butter
1 cup granulated sugar
4 large eggs
1 tbsp. baking powder
2 cups 2% milk
2 cups cornmeal
2 cups all-purpose flour
1 cup shredded white cheddar cheese
1 cup shredded yellow cheddar cheese
1 tsp. table salt
canola or vegetable oil spray,
  for greasing

SASSY
SAUCES

Adding an extra pop of color and flavor, sauces such as Red Pepper Coulis, Sherry Mushroom, and Demiglace play a spectacular supporting role alongside the loaf creations in this book.

TMB SPECIAL SAUCE

Servings: 8 to 10

This is one spectacularly special sauce. Tangy, a little sweet, and pretty as a peach, this creamy addition goes great with just about any meatloaf recipe, but definitely with No Buns About It Burger Loaf.

For the TMB Special Sauce
1½ cups mayonnaise
1 cup plus 2 tbsp. ketchup
2 tbsp. granulated sugar
1 tbsp. red wine vinegar
1 tsp. Worcestershire sauce
½ tsp. Tabasco sauce

TO MAKE

• Whisk together all the ingredients in a bowl with a wire whisk until smooth. Serve slightly chilled.

Halfway between a dressing and a sauce, this recipe is universally popular with our customers. Up to now, what's in it has been a secret: no one has ever guessed all the ingredients correctly!

SHERRY MUSHROOM SAUCE

Servings: 6 to 8

Rich with the flavors of dry sherry and white mushrooms, this sauce is a lovely complement to several meatloaf creations including El Loafo del Fuego. And who says you can't enjoy a sip or two of sherry while the sauce cooks to perfection?

TO MAKE

- In a saucepan, melt the butter and cook the mushrooms for about 15 minutes until browned and the liquid has evaporated. Add the sherry and bring to a boil. Continue boiling, stirring occasionally, until all the liquid has evaporated. Add the prepared demiglace (follow the package instructions) and simmer for about 5 to 10 minutes, or until the sauce thickens slightly, coating the back of a spoon. Season with salt and pepper and serve hot.

For the Sherry Mushroom Sauce
2 tbsp. unsalted butter
2¼ cups thinly sliced white mushrooms
1 cup very dry sherry
2 cups prepared demiglace powder (available from some culinary specialty stores and online)
coarse sea salt and freshly ground black pepper, to taste

DEMIGLACE

Servings: 6 to 8

Perk up a prepared demiglace with sautéed vegetables
and red wine. I prefer a Cabernet, although any dry
red wine will work. Taste it and you'll see how this
rich and elegant demiglace brings out the best in
The Mother Loaf, or any other meatloaf.

For the Demiglace
2 tbsp. unsalted butter
½ cup finely diced yellow onion
¼ cup finely diced celery
¼ cup finely diced carrot
1 cup dry red wine
2 cups prepared demiglace powder
(available from some culinary
specialty stores and online)
1 tsp. Worcestershire sauce
coarse sea salt and freshly ground
black pepper, to taste

TO MAKE

• In a saucepan, melt the butter and cook the onion, celery, and
carrot for about 15 minutes until browned. Add the red wine and
bring to a boil. Continue boiling, stirring occasionally, until all liquid
has evaporated. Add the prepared demiglace (follow the package
instructions) and bring to a simmer. Whisk in the Worcestershire
sauce with a fork or wire whisk and continue to simmer for about
5 to 10 minutes, or until the sauce thickens slightly, coating the
back of a spoon. Using a fine-mesh strainer, strain the vegetables
from the demiglace. Season with salt and pepper and serve warm.

SOUR CREAM LIME SAUCE

Servings: 8 to 10

Fresh lime juice and cilantro are the secrets to this refreshing sour cream-based sauce. And garlic doesn't hurt either. Try it with Holy Moly Chicken Frijole or choose your favorite southwestern creation.

TO MAKE

- Whisk together the sour cream, lime juice, cilantro, and garlic in a bowl with a fork or wire whisk until smooth. Season with salt. Cover with plastic wrap and store in the refrigerator until ready to serve. Serve chilled.

For the Sour Cream Lime Sauce
2 cups sour cream
¼ cup strained fresh lime juice
1 tbsp. chopped fresh cilantro
1 tsp. crushed garlic
fine sea salt, to taste

CRANBERRY SAUCE

Servings: 6 to 8

Sweet and tangy at the same time! This is
perfect with Herby Turkey Loaf. And I also like
it with Nutty Veggie Loaf or just by itself!

TO MAKE

- In a saucepan, bring the sugar, water, and orange juice to a boil, stirring to dissolve the sugar. Add the fresh and dried cranberries, mix well, and simmer for about 7 to 10 minutes until the cranberries soften, stirring frequently—be careful not to overcook. Let cool, or enjoy hot.

For the Cranberry Sauce
1 cup granulated sugar
½ cup water
½ cup fresh orange juice
2⅓ cups whole fresh cranberries,
   fresh or frozen
½ cup dried cranberries

RED PEPPER COULIS

Servings: 6 to 8

A surprisingly complex coulis from simple and easily obtained ingredients, this chunky sauce goes so well with meatless varieties, like Yentl Lentl Loaf. And it's perfect for Yentl Lentl Loafies, too.

TO MAKE

- Blend together all the ingredients with a food processor or immersion blender—it need not be perfectly smooth; tiny pieces of sun-dried tomatoes and roasted bell peppers will add desirable texture. Season with salt and pepper.

For the Red Pepper Coulis
2 cups drained roasted red bell
  peppers from a jar or can
⅓ cup sun-dried tomatoes in oil
1 tbsp. minced garlic
2 tbsp. extra virgin olive oil
2 tbsp. chopped fresh basil
1 tsp. granulated sugar
coarse sea salt and freshly ground
  black pepper, to taste

LEMON-DILL SAUCE

Servings: 6 to 8

Creamy and a bit tart, this lemony yogurt-based sauce blends with dill and black pepper to make a perfect match for Omega-3 Loaf.

Of the aromatics, dill is one of the less used, which is a pity, as its taste—a little sweet, a little aniseedy— is delicate and unusual. I've specified dried dill because it can be hard to find fresh, but if you see some fresh for sale, snap it up; you'll enjoy it even more.

TO MAKE

• Whisk together all the ingredients in a bowl with a fork or wire whisk until smooth. Cover with plastic wrap and store in the refrigerator until ready to serve. Serve chilled.

For the Lemon–Dill Sauce
1 cup mayonnaise
1 cup unsweetened plain yogurt
¼ cup strained fresh lemon juice
2 tsp. dried dill
2 tsp. granulated sugar
1 tsp. fine sea salt

SCALLION SOUR CREAM

Servings: 8 to 10

Who doesn't love an indulgent dollop of sour cream alongside something savory? Perfect for cooling down anything spicy, the scallions add a hint of new flavor to an already wonderful dining companion. Enjoy it with Chili Chili Bang Bang or Rootin' for Barley Loaf.

TO MAKE

- Whisk together the sour cream, milk, scallions, and garlic in a bowl with a fork or wire whisk. Season with salt and pepper. Cover with plastic wrap and store in the refrigerator until ready to serve. Serve chilled.

For the Scallion Sour Cream
2 cups sour cream
¾ cup 2% milk
½ cup chopped scallions
½ tsp. crushed garlic
fine sea salt and freshly ground
   black pepper, to taste

TZATZIKI

Servings: 6 to 8

This tangy cucumber sauce gets its zip from garlic, lemon juice, and just the right amount of black pepper. Refreshing and light, it goes great with pita, vegetables, and of course, meatloaf. Serve it up with the Lamb-A-Licious Loaf for a perfect pair.

TO MAKE

• Whisk together all the ingredients in a bowl with a fork or wire whisk. Season with salt and pepper. Cover with plastic wrap and store in the refrigerator until ready to serve. Serve chilled.

For the Tzatziki
2 cups unsweetened plain yogurt
¾ cup sliced and quartered cucumber
2 tbsp. chopped fresh mint
1½ tbsp. crushed garlic, or to taste
fine sea salt and freshly ground
   black pepper

INDEX

Acknowledgments

This book is so much more than my recipes. It's a celebration of creativity, a commitment to excellence, and a tribute to one very special food that shaped my life.

I salute Team Meatloaf, my ever-loyal and talented team of meatloaf-makers. Creating and perfecting new recipes is a group effort and as always, Team Meatloaf rose to the occasion. A special nod to Samantha Gordon for her ability to keep things going in the kitchen and make meatloaf sing on paper, to Kevin Quinn for his constancy and calm during all the frenzy, and to Sabrina Sitkoski for her culinary wizardry.

And were it not for dear friends Mary Dale Walters, Diane Salucci, and Nancy Bishop, I'd have forgotten a comma, misplaced a modifier or not known how to envision what my very own book could be. And thanks to John Habib, my nephew, always my cheerleader and a loving inspiration for recipes, quirky names and just about everything.

Then there's Judy Plummer; I simply could not have pulled this first book together without her ability to transform my recipes into cookbook form, enthusiasm for 900 ways to make meatloaf, and precious gift for making me laugh.

I wouldn't have gotten here though without incredible support during those early business-building years. My gratitude to my chef consultant, Mike Sodaro, my first banker, Adam O'Sullivan, brand creators Rae Stith, Kris Clemons and Levi Borreson, Jim Gracia, my general contractor, and to dear friends, advisors and tasters: Stacey and Tony Layzell, Ethel Duble, Heather Turk, Betty Latson, (and John, Diane, Judy and Mary Dale, of course). Thanks to my family (including my nieces and nephews who say I'm their cool aunt and love that I take risks), and especially Carole Berk, who is always by my side helping me flourish and appreciate the journey.

Thanks to the editorial and creative experts at Ivy Press with a special thank you to Tom Kitch, Sophie Collins, and Jo Richardson for their expertise, guidance, and lovely English accents.